More Than Words

More Than Words

Child-Centered Lessons for
Connecting Life and Literacy

by the author of *Doing Words*
Katie Johnson

Zephyr Press
Tucson, Arizona

More Than Words
Child-Centered Lessons for Connecting Life and Literacy
Grades PreK–3

©1995 by Katherine Johnson

Printed in the United States of America
ISBN 1-56976-016-0

Cover design: David Fischer
Design: Daniel Miedaner
Typesetting: Casa Cold Type, Inc.

Zephyr Press
P.O. Box 66006
Tucson, Arizona 85728-6006

Library of Congress Cataloging-in-Publication Data
Johnson, Katie.
  More than words : a child-centered model for connecting life and
literacy / Katie Johnson.
    p. cm.
  Includes bibliographical references.
  ISBN 1-56976-016-0
  1. Reading (Elementary)—United States—Language experience
approach. 2. Language arts (Elementary)—United States. I. Title.
LB1573.33.J65 1995
372.4'14044—dc20   95-12514

To Leah and Celia
with thanks for letting me watch them learn this language

Introduction

Raison d'être

After the publication of my first book, *Doing Words* (1987), I began to visit many schools other than my own school in Maine. I talked with teachers about Doing Words and worked in their classrooms Doing Words with their students. I talked with teachers about doing writing, and spent time with their students writing—especially revising! Since I had stopped using a basal reader myself in the early 1980s, I began to talk and demonstrate, too, about literature, and literature-as-reading, and reading and writing all through the curriculum.

The indefinable and courageous shift now known as whole language was just beginning, and I found teachers all over New England hungry, not only for ideas—teachers are always hungry for ideas—but also for something new: a validation of themselves as powerful decision-makers in and for their own classrooms and schools. In 1990 I left Maine and my own first grade, moved to Washington to watch my grandchildren grow, and began to work with teachers and children in classrooms all over the country. I have watched the self-esteem of teachers and their students grow and grow as they commit themselves to child-centered teaching, to integrated curriculum, to wholeness in their students' school lives.

Often teachers say after these sessions, "I'll just buy your book, and all these ideas and strategies you've done with us will be in it, right?" And I have to say, "No," because *Doing Words* deals pretty exclusively with Doing Words, with asides and digressions about how children learn and how people look at children. In this book, I will show-and-tell the ways to do writing and reading I have learned and invented since 1987, in scenes with live teachers and children in kindergarten through third grade. I hope that these stories will give you the courage to say, "Oh, I can do that!"

Contents

1

At the Beginning: Doing Words

Movements I, II, III

"What do you want for a Word today, Angela?" I asked the next five-year-old, patting the chair next to me at the table. I had a lot of Movement I children still in this group on this December day; about half were in Movement II, and a small few in Movement III already. Not an untypical distribution.

"Theresa," replied Angela promptly as she sat down.

"Theresa," I repeated, printing it on a card of heavy tag paper about two by twelve inches. "Is Theresa your friend today?"

"She's spending the night with me tonight," Angela said. "We're gonna watch videos." She put her left hand on the upper left corner of the card, where I had written her name, to hold it down, and began to trace the letters with her right index finger. *"T, h, e, r, e, s, a,"* she murmured as she traced. "Look, teacher, there are two *es.*"

"What do you want for a Word today, Angela?" I asked the next five-year-old, patting the chair next to me at the table.

"Right, Angela," I said, delighted. "Read me this Word, please."

"Theresa," Angela read, already out of the chair, taking her Word to read to two friends and put into the basket. And here came John, in Movement II.

"Good morning, John," I greeted him. "How goes it today?" I could see Angela, reading her card to Theresa. Her next task was to send someone else to Do Words with me.

"Good," answered John. "I know what I want today, about my brother, remember I told you."

"Yes, I certainly do," I answered. "Bradley had to have his tonsils out, didn't he? Was that your Word yesterday?"

"Yep, and today I want 'My brother is coming home today.'"

"Oh, I'm glad," I said, writing John's name in the upper left corner of a longer oaktag card. "My brother is coming home today," I said slowly as I printed the words. "Read this, please, John."

John slid the card nearer to himself and read the words. I framed them as he read, my thumb and forefinger making a kind of mouth above each word as he said it.

"Super! That's a long sentence, too. Trace the words for me please, and let's see—can you show me which word says *brother*?"

John put his finger under *My* and slid it along the whole card, saying softly, "My brother is coming home today;" he stopped with his hand under *today*. Today he didn't stop at *brother*; the next day I would ask him to identify a specific word in that day's sentence and if he didn't, I would sweep the card from left to right myself and show him that word. Some children go right to word-for-word reading in Movement II, some don't. It doesn't matter. It comes.

> "You sure can read that whole thing," I said admiringly. "Now it's time to trace. Please do it all today."

"You sure can read that whole thing," I said admiringly. "Now it's time to trace. Please do it all today." As John obligingly traced all the letters on the card, from the left side of it to the right side before he, too, took the card to read to two friends and put into the basket, I made a mental note. John had been in Movement II for not quite a week and was remembering his sentences just fine. The differentiation of which word was which would come soon; that knowledge is an important part of Movement II.

Angela had sent—surprise, surprise—Theresa. Theresa was also in Movement I. She had brought all her Word cards with her to read to me, because it was a Blue day and Theresa was a Blue. Every day I heard all the Words of the children whose color day it was. (The color groups are simply for management, so that I have a small set of people to concentrate on every day, to hear read their Words, to hear read at reading time, to choose for show and tell, to choose as helpers, to let line up first, and so forth.) The children read all their Words every day to another child, but I hear each child once a week to be sure that the Words in the collection still have important meaning. If they don't, I take them away, as with one of Theresa's.

Theresa kept her cards, as all the children did that year, in a folder that had been stapled together and decorated by its owner. For reasons I didn't understand, the district central office had ordered many many boxes of file folders and none of the large manila envelopes that I prefer for keeping Words. I appropriated enough for the class to have two each, one to use in the early Movements of doing Words, one for Movement VI. Theresa's folder was covered with crayoned flowers, the kind that are made with four or five looping strokes in a circle for the petals and a smaller circle inside for the center, with two matching green blobs for leaves on the stem holding it up. Most of her flowers were pink, yellow, or light blue. Theresa is all pastels.

"Hi, Theresa," I said. "Ready to read your Words to me?"

"Yes," she said, laying down her folder carefully on the table and reaching carefully into it, pulling out all her cards. She tapped them together, making a tidy stack, setting the folder aside so that its lower edge was aligned with the tabletop. She began to read, turning each card over after she read it.

"*Mother. Caroline. Angela. Smokey. Daddy. rabbit. bus station. Halloween. Christmas. John. Mary Ellen. pizza.*" The next word was *mascara*. Theresa looked at the card. There was a silence. I waited. "I forget," said Theresa. She looked at me.

"That's okay," I said. "Put it at the bottom of your pile, and we'll do it last."

She slid the card carefully under her tidy stack and continued. "*Birthday. Grandma. fair. ballerina. rainbow. Janie. puzzle. Tiffany. Disney World. Barbie*" and there came *mascara* again. Again she looked at me.

"Well," I said, "this one doesn't seem to be very important to you." I put my hand on it.

"No," said Theresa anxiously. "I'll think of it."

I waited a little, counting slowly to twenty in my head. "It was about something special your mother let you wear," I said. Of course I knew the provenance of all the Words in the room, because I had written them on

> **"I'll put it over on my desk for now, and when you remember, just go get it and read it to me. I'll just leave it on my desk."**

the cards after a minute of talking with each child every day. This story came only from a few days before, since the last Blue day, so it was certainly possible that she hadn't ever remembered it.

"Ballet shoes?" said Theresa tentatively.

"No," I said. "I don't think you've ever told me about ballet shoes."

She looked at it again. I put my hand on the card and she tugged it back. "No! I'll remember it!" she exclaimed. "Don't take it away!"

"No, no," I said quickly, "I'll put it over on my desk for now, and when you remember, just go get it and read it to me. I'll just leave it on my desk."

She agreed to this option, and put the rest of the cards back into her envelope.

"That's a lot of Words you know, Theresa," I said. "Pretty nifty! What is your Word for today?" Picking up my marker and a new card, I looked at her expectantly.

"*Jumprope*," she said. Who cares about ballet shoes, anyway? I asked myself.

"Tell me about the jumprope," I said invitingly while I uncapped my marker and wrote 'Theresa' in the upper left corner of the card.

"Gramma got me a new one and it's pink," she explained.

"Lucky you!" I said, printing. "Here it is then, watch: *j, u, m, p, r, o, p, e*," I said, naming the letters. "Trace it, please."

She traced the letters with her forefinger, saying them as she traced, parroting the way I had written and named them.

"Now what do you do?" I asked.

"I'll read it to two people and put it in the basket," she said.

"Great. And would you also send Nicholas and Penny over here?"

Nicholas and Penny were the two in this class, so far, who were in Movement III. They came with their writing books, because in Movement III children transcribe the sentence with a pencil. In Movements III and IV of Doing Words, the writing book is merely four or five sheets of lined writing paper stapled together with a cover of some sort (a piece of wallpaper or construction paper will do fine). The words and sentences of Movements I and II have gone home in the decorated folder.

> "Tell me what this says," I invited him. Sometimes I say, "Read this," which is the same thing, after all.

Nicholas got there first. "Hi, Nicholas, what's your Word today?" I always say *word* even when it's a sentence, because the whole idea of *something important, something key,* first emerged in a single captioning word in Movement I. Now the key thing, cast as a sentence as it also was in Movement II, will be printed, but it is still to each child, each day, *something important*.

"You mean a sentence, Teacher," Nicholas reminded me helpfully. He laid his writing book on the table, and I reached for some small strips of the same kind of paper that was in his writing book.

"Right," I agreed. I opened my marker, put an *N* on one corner of the strip and capped the marker again to concentrate on Nicholas.

"My dog is having puppies and I watched them come out before school." Nicholas was absolutely ready with this report.

"You did! What was it like?"

"Well, it was kinda yukky, you know?" He squirmed a little. "There were three puppies out before I had to get on the bus, and Mom thought there might be six. I can't wait to get home tonight and see 'em."

"I guess!" I agreed. "What a neat thing to get to see, Nicholas!" I uncapped the marker and asked again, "What are you writing today?"

"I saw three puppies get born this morning," said Nicholas. I began to write, accepting this revision of his first statement. As much as he loves the dog, the key thing about this birthing event was his own presence as observer.

"Tell me what this says," I invited him. Sometimes I say, "Read this," which is the same thing, after all. While he traced *puppies* I turned to Penny.

"Good morning, Ms. Penny," I greeted her. "How are you today?"

"Good," she said. "Guess what, my birthday's in three weeks and I'm gonna have a party, too!"

Penny's sentence emerged as "My birthday is in three weeks." I printed it, then slid my hand along beneath the words. "Read this, please," I said, and she did. "What's the most important word here today?" I asked.

With a happy look she replied, "*Birthday*," found it on the card, and traced it while I looked back at Nicholas, now copying his sentence neatly into his writing book. These little books, full of the captions of the pieces of the child's life, are read with a friend every morning before the new sentence is entered, and when they are filled up they go home to be read to the family, the neighbors, and anyone else who happens in. They read like a list of headlines, which is perfectly understandable, although occasionally there is some continuity. It wouldn't surprise me if Penny's sentence the next day were "I can't wait 'til my birthday."

These first three Movements will carry kindergartners along from October to at least April and sometimes all the way to the end of the year. Children who Do Words see their own speech—words and sentences—in standard English and spelling every day; they read it several times; they learn the names of the letters and how they are made; they learn that names have capitals and sentences have periods, and that writing and reading in English go from left to right. They learn to print, to read, to share, to talk. The power of their commitment to what is important to them is the driving force behind all this learning. Young children, as we all know, have immense energy. They harness it to Doing Words and the language opens in their hands and heads: they own it.

I always prefer to Do Words at the beginning of the day for at least three reasons. First of all, most of the children are at their freshest (although some few only wake up after snack, it seems), and the center work that accompanies Word time is good for exploration, discovery, and transition from home to school. Second, I get a chance to check in with everybody, to hear what's going on with each one. Third, if I need an idea for something we need to work further on right now, often the content of the Words will provide that. Some days, for example, as many as six Movement II and III children will have sentences using an *-ing* verbal form or reporting on a common event, such as the circus.

The first thing that happens in Word time is reading, with a partner, the entire folder or envelope of cards. The children who have writing books instead of cards read the whole book. (This is one reason those books have so few pages; the other reason is that when the books are full they go home, and they'll get home faster if they are only four or five pages long.) During this buzzing exchange I am finding the cards and strips and markers and calling the first one of the set of children who will read with me today. After I hear each of those children and give each of them a new Word, I call or send for each of the others, who will get just a new Word. After and before a child has worked with me, he or she may do one or some of the activities around the room.

After every five or six children, I try to leave the marker in charge of the next child and circle the room, encouraging and monitoring. Then I return to where I was and go on. After getting a new card, a child in Movements I or II must go read it to two friends. After writing the sentence in Movement III, the child must go read the writing—the child's writing in the book, not the strip I wrote on—to two friends. Then I put the day's cards and the writing books in a certain place, which might be a special basket or box, or it might just be a spot near the teacher. The strips from Movement III can go home or be stuffed in a desk or a pocket, or even tossed.

After everyone has a new Word, including me, we clean up and come to the circle. I bring the basket and sit in the circle myself and start the cards and books, one at a time, around the circle. "Please take yours as it goes by, and put it on the floor in front of you. If it isn't yours, please pass it along." This takes a shorter time each day, of course, and the children's connection to all this print is so much greater than if I give each student his or her word myself that I don't worry about a few extra minutes. Besides, nearly everyone gets to see nearly everyone else's Words.

Then, when the floor in front of each child has a card or a book on it, and there are no more strips or books floating around the circle, we read.

> **"Please take yours as it goes by, and put it on the floor in front of you. If it isn't yours, please pass it along."**

"I'm going to choose the best and quietest listener to read first," I say softly; after that one has read the next one does, and so on around the circle. If we have a lot of time, especially in first grade, I ask each reader to choose the next one, but the time constraints of half-day kindergarten seldom permit that.

For the remaining four or five minutes we have a little lesson, which can go absolutely anywhere. I might say, "If you have a Word that is a name, slide it out into the middle," and those words would be read again; I might ask for all the words that are animals, or family members, or alive, or not alive—various kinds of classification; I might ask for all the Words with a *t* in them, or a *t* at the beginning, or whatever—various kinds of phonetic observation; or (especially in Movements II and III) "If you have an apostrophe in your Word today, hold it up"; or an *-ing* or a compound, or anything else that we can observe about the structure of the language. Sometimes I do it backwards, that is, draw a conclusion instead of look at examples:

"Jessica, Tony M., Maria, Heather, and John, please slide your cards out for a minute. Now who can see something these children all have?" And someone will say periods, and someone will say capitals at the beginning, and some will say something that's true about them all that I didn't notice, because I was focused on the apostrophes (in *I'm, He's, Jason's, I'll* and *I'm*, respectively).

It's always safer and more rewarding to ask an open-ended rather than a one-answer-possible question!

Then we put all these things away in boxes and desks and go out to play.

Every day each child has the teacher's undivided attention for a minute or two (slightly longer if, as in Theresa's case, it's her day to read all the words or sentences she has collected). Every day the teacher has a minute or two to concentrate on each child, focusing on her use of language but certainly noticing other, often nonacademic, aspects of her life. Stories that might be too "big" for show-and-tell surface here, even if they don't end up as Words; neglect or physical problems emerge during this minute; here, accomplishments in the language can be noticed and delighted in, as well. It's a little oasis of discovery and bonding on all sides.

In a more rarefied and nonverbal interpretation, Doing Words says to each child, "You are important. What you think and connect to and believe in are important. What is inside your heart and head is so important, in fact, that we will use it for your reading and writing instead of other material not anywhere near as important to you."

And Doing Words says to the teacher, "Here is all the phonics and grammar and penmanship and visual discrimination practice you and the children will ever need." Tracing and naming the letters in the words, then reading them and writing them, will teach the children all they need about letter recognition, letter formation, left-to-right progression, the definitions of *word* and *sentence*, punctuation, capitalization, and the odd things that English does, as well as incidentally teaching them that they can read and write.

Children have a lot of energy for their own "stuff." Doing Words turns that energy into power for all of you in the classroom, so all of you may use it to teach and to learn. The name of the game is *connecting,* the constant connecting of the child to the print and life of the classroom and the world *from the inside out,* that is, through the child's own commitment to the idea or book or words or counting or song or butterfly or map or weather at hand, in that child's own life. All the child-centered ways a teacher has of running a classroom and a school make connections in just this way, watching the children all the time, learning how they are learning so that teaching can be more effective and more apropos every minute, so that learning will be ever more likely to happen.

I begin the connecting with what Sylvia Ashton-Warner called the "one-look word," powerful personal images from and for each child. I begin by Doing Words.

Notes: Doing Words

> When we do words we take the images that are important to a child and give them to him to read and write. Organic words are the captions to the pictures in the mind of the child; when we give such a caption to a child to read and write and keep and remember, a bridge is laid between the world of his own person and the outer world in which his personality must function. (Johnson 1987, 4)

By Doing Words, young children become eager readers and writers. They learn the rules of standard English as they read and write their own words, their own sentences, their own stories. Because what they write is so important, they will want to be sure that others can read it. The power of the Word carries over to their use of the language itself.

Use that power.

In Doing Words children write and read in six movements, using the power of their own personal images. For the complete outline, with lots of examples, read *Doing Words* (Johnson 1987).

Movement I: An important or key Word, special to each child, chosen daily and written by the teacher on a card after conversation with each child (one minute per child will do it), to trace and read and share and remember. The child traces with a finger

and later also names the letters in the daily Word, reads it to others, reads it in a class sharing circle, and builds a collection of forty Words, which are read daily to a friend and weekly to the teacher. The Word is removed from the collection if it no longer has power.

Movement II: An important sentence, to read and trace and share and remember. The procedure is the same as in Movement I, including conversation, tracing, reading, sharing daily in the circle.

Movement III: Exactly like Movement II, except for the tracing, because the child prints the sentence in a personal notebook and reads from that notebook in the circle, not from the strip the teacher wrote on.

Movement IV: Exactly like III, except the teacher writes the child's sentence(s) on a personal word list called a *retrieval card.*

Movement V: Long, mostly continuing stories written with the aid of a personal dictionary. This movement can last several months and be the context for much teaching.

Movement VI: Like Movement V, but adding the revision and editing of writing process.

2

Writing and Inventing in Stereo

When I was a little girl, my first-grade teacher sold my parents a set of the World Book Encyclopedia. My parents didn't buy it for me—my older sister was in sixth grade at the time. When I got old enough to take the volumes down without dropping them on my foot, I liked to look at the pictures; mostly I was fascinated by the part, at the very beginning of each volume, that showed the development of the letter itself, from a picture through various shapes to our current way of writing it. The Phoenicians were always credited with the earliest form; when I asked my mother who they were she told me they sailed all over the sea with things to sell in big clay jars. I wondered if they had letters, like my stamp set, in one of their clay jars, too.

The letters of the alphabet began with drawing, as indeed did all written communication. Think of cave paintings and petroglyphs, so very long ago, or the marks made on the doors of the houses where babies should be spared. Drawing is still used to communicate, as newspaper cartoons show every day and as the little pale green figures and little red-orange hands show at cross-walks. Drawing is still the beginning of writing.

Leah, age two, asks for a pen and paper and says she is going to do some writing. She makes very little marks all over the paper, and then says, "What's that?" Sometimes, lately, she says as she is doing this, "Once upon a time . . . "

Trucks and cars and curling smoke from exhaust pipes cover Todd's paper, and next to some of the vehicles are labels: *PS* next to the one with the siren lights on top, red and blue; *FRK* next to the long red one; *SOB* next to the one with long skis under its black body. This is a catalog with labels, although only the police car, the fire truck, and the snowmobile have them. Todd is five and, as we would have gotten away with saying twenty-five years ago, he is all boy.

"IWTTOMIVS," Karen, also five, reported on Monday, on a page with a drawing of herself and her sister and a house. "I went to my Grammy's," she read from the journal entry when asked. "I got this new dress, too," she added, twirling around in it. Later she added to her writing a picture of the dress, pink bow and all, and labeled it "MIJS."

"ISO PEZDNTB AT ROZGDRN HEGAV MOM APIN. VBOD CLAPT IFLTPR," wrote Jamie, age six, in his journal in school. His teacher knew that he and his mother had gone to Washington for a vacation, but she didn't know that the President had given his mother a pin in the Rose Garden. As the story continued orally, it became clear that it was a fantasy—except that he really "felt proud" of his mom.

In the waiting room of the clinic, Steven and Ana stood at the table reaching over and across each other to grab the bright markers in the bucket. Ana used each color carefully, drawing a series of arches with each one, so that her paper was becoming a multicolored rainbow. This was the same picture she had drawn every day with the markers since she first came here two months ago. Lately she'd been trying to put the colors in order, so there was a repeated pattern of colors. Steven, with a different style, ripped off the cap of one marker, made a slash mark across the paper with one color, threw the uncapped marker onto the table, grabbed another and slashed color, then took up the black one and scribbled across all of it. Steven held the markers in his fist, vertically, and bore down hard; several of their parallelogram-points were mashed and split.

All of these children—Leah, Todd, Karen, Jamie, Steven, Ana—are in the process of acquiring print for their own use. They have already learned one of the two fundamental elements of the English language, namely, that it is theirs and that they can use it to say important things about their own lives. The children in the earliest stages know that marks go on paper (Steven), might be something (Ana), or might mean something (Leah). They are not in school yet. The others are working in school on understanding the sound-symbol correspondences which make writing work.

Given the various degrees of emphasis on spoken and written language in various cultures represented in our schools, it is not possible to assume that all children have been read to before they come to school, nor that anyone has listened and echoed their efforts to put the sounds of the language together. Leah's parents often talk about rhymes as they occur in conversation, or the unusual sounds of words in stories they read, nightly and often daily, as well. Leah has any number of crayons, markers, pads of paper, paint, and chalk available to her for graphic experimentation of all kinds. Her family celebrates reading and writing. Steven's family, on the other hand, does not.

His adults have not hovered over his utterances and nudged them into mainstream language, nor have they encouraged him to make writing and drawing a part of his play.

Leah will come to school, as Jamie and Karen did, knowing all the letters by name, knowing what reading is and what books are, knowing how to put some of what is in her head onto paper. Ana and

Children all reinvent the language, beginning whenever their home culture makes the understanding of print either intriguing or routine.

Steven will not. It's a difference in culture that, unfortunately, the schools until very recently have not bothered to address. As Lisa Delpit puts it, to the acquisition of language at school "Different children bring different ways of construing the world as a result of the cultures they grow up in" (Delpit 1991, 543).

Children all reinvent the language, beginning whenever their home culture makes the understanding of print either intriguing or routine. It is at home that children learn the first part of literacy, speaking, and learn how their grownups regard and use print. In rural settings, where life is often lived much more out-of-doors, the world of print may have much less interest and importance in the preschooler's life. Particularly in cities, preschool children whose families do not belong to what Lisa Delpit calls the "culture of power" have been treated differently by their elders than are those children within that culture of power. School in America is based on print from the very beginning; children who have less experience with it are at an automatic disadvantage regardless of why they have less experience.

Shirley Brice Heath (1983) relates language interactions among children and grownups in the families she studied. The models differ greatly among families. Children learn to talk, of course, in whatever language or dialect their home grownups use with them. What Delpit and Heath also show, though, is that the ways in which literacy and language development are encouraged by those grownups vary according to culture.

Leah's grownups, for example, read to her every night and every day. They talk to her and make admiring sounds about her squiggles. Ana's grownups have books, but being read to is not part of her ritual. When Leah and Ana go to school, their teachers will assume that they both know about books, that stories come out of books, and that print tells the stories; Ana won't know, however, and will be at a disadvantage in terms of the expectations of the school.

Ever-growing numbers of children from various cultures make up our schools, and the variety of preschool literacy experiences these children bring to school is mind-boggling. If the school bases its expectations on the worldview and literacy pattern of the culture of power, children who do not construe the world in the same way will have to learn how to do so, when they get to school if not before. For children whose first language isn't any kind of English, the cultural differences are clearer, though no less important, than for American Indian and African American children. It is a clearer issue, actually, for children whose language isn't any kind of English, standard or not. The whole problem is enormously more complicated within the deaf community—is Sign to be treated as another language, with the implication that the deaf belong to another culture? Deaf language will be explored further in chapter 5. Early literacy experiences, then, may have to take place in school, making the teacher's day even more exciting.

In Harriet's Seattle kindergarten classroom there are almost as many print-awareness backgrounds as there are children. Twenty-seven children are sitting around a large open square of tables. They have white paper and black markers and are busily drawing pictures of whatever they want to draw. Some are labeling, too, and some are making writing to go with the drawing. Because it is an October morning, there are a lot of witches and Ninjas and pumpkins. Harriet is going around the tables, talking with the children about what they are doing, putting the date at the top of the paper with the child's name. Sometimes she writes a few words to tell what is going on in the picture if the child asks her to do so; mostly her function is to see and date the drawings and to let the children know, by her very presence and interest, that this work is important.

> **"What a lot of interesting things we have to share today," she beams at the group. "Here is Gustavo's paper first—tell us about it, please, Gustavo."**

Whenever a child finishes drawing, Harriet puts the paper in a folder she is carrying. The children go to other activities, then, blocks and dress-up and Play Doh and games. When the tables are empty and her folder is full, she walks around observing their activities and reminding them that they will be coming to sharing soon. Cleanup follows, then they all arrive in a place on the rug together. She sits down, too, and opens the folder.

"What a lot of interesting things we have to share today," she beams at the group. "Here is Gustavo's paper first—tell us about it, please, Gustavo."

A tiny boy stands up and points to the paper she is holding up for all to see. "It's dinosaurs, see. All dinosaurs."

"Thank you, Gustavo," says Harriet after a short wait to see if he has anything more to add, and Gustavo sits down again. "Next is Susannah's drawing."

Susannah stands up, tossing a lot of curly hair off her neck. "That my baby sister, she in her crib and she's throw her doll at me," says Susannah.

"What for?" asks Maria. "Why'd she throw it at you?"

Susannah shrugs. The little wait, then "Thank you," from Harriet, as she holds up another drawing.

This showing and talking about each drawing goes on for a good fifteen minutes and gives everyone a chance to tell about his or her drawing if he or she has anything more to say. Sometimes, to be sure, the child has "drawn it out," and has nothing more to say. That is fine. Occasionally Harriet says something about a drawing, such as, "My, that looks just like a Stegosaurus," or "You've been making lots of trucks this week; you certainly know a lot about them," or some other encouraging and admiring statement.

Harriet calls this activity her writers' workshop, and she does it most days of the week, in the middle of the morning before recess. The pictures are wildly various in terms of fine-motor control, completeness, and artistic merit. Most of these five- and six-year-old children have made no attempt to put any letters on the page; the letters of those who have made an attempt are all over the place, both in position and formation.

In this group are many different home languages, including two American Indian languages, standard English, and the English dialects present in this diverse urban environment. Harriet's classroom will offer many of these children their first opportunity to be directed or even encouraged to do anything with marks on paper. That's why Harriet does this activity all together around the table; many would not choose this activity on their own because it is unfamiliar.

In Mrs. Peterson's kindergarten in a different part of the city, on the other hand, the children move around centers for twenty minutes, and one of the centers is the Journal Table. Each child has a folder in a big decorated box, and on the table are a date stamp and pad, many kinds of paper, and many small tubs of crayons and markers. During his or her turn at the table, each child has to make lots of decisions connected with the content of the entry for that day: what kind of paper, what to write with, what to draw about, how to write about it, and other questions, such as "What color are clouds in my mind today?" can be fearsomely important.

The children put these drawings-with-writing right into their own folders. Some days Mrs. Peterson finds time to get the drawings out, pass them around, and ask the children to share their day's work. Mrs. Peterson calls this activity her writers' workshop, and asks that the children do it at least three times a week, signing themselves in on a laminated chart.

The children in her class feel very much at home with writing and drawing; when Mrs. Peterson introduced this activity, they recognized its elements from their lives at home and at preschool. Twenty-two of the twenty-three come from families in the mainstream culture.

These two versions of writers' workshop, a.k.a. journal writing, have in common the most important element: ownership. Each child in Harriet's and Mrs. Peterson's rooms will choose what he or she will do in this writing, drawing time.

In addition to the obvious differences in the pool of the children in the room, two differences stand out: The teacher's time to rejoice and take public notice of each child's work is absent from Mrs. Peterson's room, as is the daily, required, expected sharing with the other children. Grownup and peer validation of the children is very much part of life in Harriet's class. Very generally speaking, the children in Mrs. Peterson's class have already learned how to share and that grownups care about their work at home. This is new stuff for many in Harriet's class.

> **Writing and drawing become comfortable only when they are routine, routine, routine, and children must feel comfortable and safe about them in order to succeed in American schools.**

As well as being an exciting and pride-building activity for all children, then, this nearly daily workshop event is also a chance for the children who have had no preschool practice or home practice doing this kind of work to get to do some of it. Writing and drawing become comfortable only when they are routine, routine, routine, and children must feel comfortable and safe about them in order to succeed in American schools. This situation may not be fair, or right, but it is the way of things just now. Particularly in large classrooms with children of many heritages and lifestyles, it is essential to make time for a writers' workshop. Begin with drawing for those who need to draw as their first understanding of what writing is, then go on from there, to arrive at a competency with written language and spelling. There are ways and ways to do this. Mrs. Peterson and Harriet provide the structure, the requirement, the tools, and that most important foundation for self-esteem, ownership. It is possible, however, to find writing workshops where providing just one other element ruins it all.

Ginger, in a different school in first grade, has a writing journal, too. Some days she writes in it, some days she doesn't. She is writing in her journal on Tuesday, "If snowflakes were colored IT wood bee a dream with froot all ovr the Plase." Snowflakes and stars of many colors drift over the whole page, and Ginger is concentrating now on the box of colored pencils, choosing her next snowflake.

Ginger's teacher writes a beginning every day on the chalkboard for the children to copy and continue in their journals, and today's is "If snowflakes were colored . . . " Ginger has excellent control over this English language of hers. After the first four words, the teacher-words she copies from the board to start her journal entry this Tuesday, Ginger finishes the sentence with perfectly clear writing, demonstrating that she has a lot of words already tucked into her memory, so this work is not stretching Ginger as much as she needs at this time in her life—not as much as Ana and Gustavo and Todd are stretching. One of the things Ginger is not being stretched to do is to decide what she wants to write about. Ginger's teacher always says,"Now children, you may write in your journals about anything you want to, but if you can't think of anything, use this idea." By putting the *but* where she does, the teacher suggests very strongly that the first half of the sentence is the wrong direction, the second half is the desirable one. *But* is a sneaky word, the way it wipes out what has just been said.

> **If, on a particular day, a particular child is having trouble coming up with an idea, the teacher's duty (and delight) is to go talk to that child!**

The message from the teacher is very clear: Ginger's not likely to have an idea of her own, and if she does it won't be as good as the teacher's. The secondary messages are even more destructive: Ginger is better off not thinking for herself, and the teacher, secretly, doesn't trust her to have ideas. If I were to tell Ginger's teacher that those are the messages she gives with her starters each day, she would deny it: then she would say, "But kids have trouble coming up with things to write about." No; teachers often have trouble believing that kids can think. If, on a particular day, a particular child is having trouble coming up with an idea, the teacher's duty (and delight) is to go talk to that child! Ask what's on his mind, ask what she had for dinner, ask how his dog is doing, ask what she's gonna do at recess! Justin's journal entry that day was to draw his favorite Ninja turtles, lovely ones—as lovely as those dreadful reptiles get. On the lines Justin had dutifully copied the chalkboard beginning and then filled up the page with words labeling things around the room: "If snowflakes were colored window door bears schedule Mrs. Smithers chalkboard January Tomorrow will be Thursday." Clearly the prompt was meaningless for Justin. If Harriet had been his teacher, she would probably have asked him about his picture and asked him if he'd like to write Ninja, asked him to tell her what letter it started with, waited while he wrote his *N* and possibly a *J* because, as she would have pointed out, *Justin* has the same sound, so his journal for that day would have been the invented spelling label for his own drawing, *NJ*.

To do the routine Harriet does is a super way to teach children who have little background with drawing or writing (remembering that for the youngest ones these are often exactly the same) what it's all about, this business of pencils, paper, and print. To talk Justin, in a very focused and discovering way, through the labeling of his own idea, is a super way to teach him what sounds and letters have to do with each other.

Ginger doesn't need the amount of direction she's getting, nor would she need the same teaching Justin needs. Their classmates are strung out along a long continuum of developing understanding and use of language. Generic writer's workshop, then, is where children are expected to do some drawing/writing every day that the center is available and the time is open (pull-out P.E. and art have a lot to answer for in terms of the fragmentation of schedules in primary classrooms—leave aside drug awareness and Smokey the Bear). Harriet's inner-city young kindergartners were helped by her around-the-table structure; Mrs. Peterson's children were continuing the kind of work Harriet's children were beginning. This work told these teachers where each child was in language acquisition.

> **Begin where the child is and take (leading, nudging, pushing, pulling, and teaching) him or her as far as possible in the time you have together.**

Mrs. Smithers's controlling prompts were not helpful to either end of her spectrum of ordinary suburban first graders. Justin didn't get it, wasn't ready, and Ginger understood that one little bit of text with no connection to herself *satisfied the teacher*. Neither child was validated or centered in himself or herself by this writing activity. (Really, any time writing is characterized as an "activity" it's almost by definition not child centered.) In its healthiest form, a writing workshop in a kindergarten or in a first grade is an opportunity for both the child and the teacher to learn about the child.

Sometimes schools and the mainstream culture in general have assumed that because Justin did not get the same literacy education at home as Leah did, he is not as bright. I have heard teachers from the mainstream culture talking about parents, often—it's their third favorite topic after kids and principals. "What is the matter with those people?" they tend to explode. "Susannah (or Peter or Darryl or Lanisha or Suzette or Maria) says her mom and dad Never read to her! What am I supposed to do? Begin at the beginning??" The answer is, as it always has been, begin where the child is and take (leading, nudging, pushing, pulling, and teaching) him or her as far as possible in the time you have together.

It is usually not the idea of children's writing that is troublesome to parents and other grownups, but the form it takes. Jamie's version of the visit to the Rose Garden was not made difficult by its fantastical nature, but by its spelling. These writings and labelings are examples of the way children use their growing understanding of print and sounds to invent their own spelling and use it as they need it to communicate in writing. Many respectable researchers, in many excellent books and articles written since 1982, have documented this strategy, known as "invented" or "developmental" spelling, and I am fascinated by the descriptions of the way children move through their reinvention of the (ghastly) English orthography and phonics system.

Since I believe in Doing Words as well as in doing writing workshops, the children I teach have a chance to see every day the language as it truly is, on their Word cards, in the sentences they copy, and in whatever spellings they ask me to write in their word bank/spelling dictionaries when they are writing extended and continuing text. They also use whatever language they are currently constructing as they do writing at a writing center and in their

reading and science responses. These experiences are wonderful for all of us—teacher, students, parents—in the primary grades. The parents get to see that the children are using real English to read and write; the teacher gets a running display of the current state of development of each child's spelling system. The students, luckiest of all, get a stereophonic wraparound of the language, the output of the speaker of the standard forms merging continuously inside their heads with the output of the speaker of their own connections of any moment. This sound system eventually unifies itself—usually around the end of first grade for children who have begun the two-tone procedure in kindergarten.

Todd, of the cars and trucks, was getting a new Word every day, and you will never guess what those Words were mostly about! *Fire truck, truck, bulldozer, police car, ambulance, backhoe.* Karen had, among her words, *Grammy* and *pink.* Their understandings of how English works (and never forget that it makes very little sense!) are being built inside each one's head out of their intuition and the power of their personal ideas.

> **Explain it. Show them. Ask them to be on the lookout at home, too, for evidence of the blending of the real and developmental worlds.**

Parents can understand this building perfectly well, if we show and tell them how their children are growing in their understanding of spelling, with samples from the children's own work. It makes much more sense than the blithe, "Oh, we're not worrying about spelling yet!" Maybe we're not, but we are certainly aware of it and parents need to know that. Most adults remember spelling very well from their own schooling. Most adults see very little that is the same about school as when they were in it, so they grasp as to a floating log at spelling which certainly, they expect, can't change. They are suspicious of what they think might mean a muddy future for Todd or Karen if either can't spell.

Explain it. Show them. Ask them to be on the lookout at home, too, for evidence of the blending of the real and developmental worlds. Use them, reassure them, rejoice with them as the progress shows up in class.

And then, in the third quarter of first grade or as soon as is logical in second grade, teach the children to be responsible for their own spelling. I believe that there is only so far that developmental spelling can go, and after that Todd and Karen, and Gustavo, too, must learn—understand? accept?—that the English language is weird, irregular, totally a mess as far as spelling is concerned. There are rules, but they are as often broken as kept, and they will probably mislead you. Even the easiest one, that a word with a silent *e* on the end will drop it when *-ing* is added, is misleading. The minute you have made sure that the children have bought that one, someone will want to write a story about canoeing! It's best to memorize. And, if you're going to memorize, it's best to memorize first the words that are of use to you.

As children past first grade work on their own writings with a personal word bank or spelling-book, teacher- or commercially made, the adults in their classroom will enter the words they need to spell as they write. I make the books out of seven sheets of ditto paper folded in half and sewn or stapled together with a tag cover; each page has a letter of the alphabet written on it. When a child needs a word she has to put the book in front of my nose open to the page the word starts with.

"I need *carving,* please," said Abby politely one day. Her book was open to *C,* showing me that she'd already made the *c* versus *k* decision.

"Can you spell *car,* Abby?" I asked.

"*C, a, r,*" she replied promptly. I wrote those letters down and looked expectantly at her.

"What do you hear next?" I asked.

"V-v-v," sounded Abby. "*V!*"

"Right," I agreed, writing it.

"And that *ing* is *i, n, g,*" Abby added nonchalantly.

"Wow," I said. "You sounded that whole thing out yourself. Good job!"

These little phonics lessons go by all the time when the children use their personal spelling books.

Children do need to learn to spell. Not first, and not unnaturally, but if they are to be literate and competent citizens, spelling correctly is part of the deal. Not that children or any other humans will spell correctly just because they've seen the words correctly. Learning to spell is immensely easier if they get to use words in their writing all the time. Spelling, like all other pieces of the literacy cake, must be meaningful.

Notes: Inventing in Stereo

Journals are personal writings, and "writings," and drawings, all undirected. No prompts are necessary, except the very generic, "You may write or draw whatever is on your mind today."

Journals can be a daily feature of school life or, if daily is not possible, they can be on another, but regular, schedule.

Journals are more fun when students use colored markers, and the child must be able to choose whether or not to use a pencil in journal work even when he or she is using pencils for Doing Words or other work.

A possible progression from preschool on with many variations often occurring in the same classroom:

- plain sheets of paper, using many colors of fat markers, one per day on a clipboard, or several sheets at a time in a teacher-bound booklet or a bought, unlined composition book; children may label their drawings if they want to, although they probably will not

- plain sheets with a base line near the bottom edges; teacher may label or write at child's dictation; skinny markers

- paper with the top half lined, the bottom half plain in teacher-bound booklets; the students write a sentence and illustrate it; any implements

- children use any implement to write in regular composition books a sentence with invented spelling

- children write with any implement using personal dictionaries and environmental print and illustrate if they want to

Send home the booklets when they are full, or the single sheets when there are as many as the child is old, with a cover letter to parents explaining that this is the work you watch most closely to evaluate how well the child is learning letter sounds, printing, and spelling. Ask the parents to rejoice in the progress of the child and to ask the child to "read" the journal pages to them. Staple the same letter to each one that goes home.

3

Language Experience in the Primary Grades

Andrew appeared one April morning with a wonderful parachute, a small one, with a heavy bolt attached to it by a string. Andrew is a very determined young man, one might even say forceful, and he told me he wanted to show everyone how the parachute worked. No no, not at recess, which was my first idea; now, right now was his ideal moment.

After some relatively reasonable conversation—Andrew was seven-and-a-half, and I was my usual forty-going-on-six—we compromised on demonstrating the parachute right after lunch count and before calendar. When it was time, we all trooped outside to the parking lot, Andrew (forcefully) arranged everyone in a circle, flew his parachute and its attendant bolt with great success and panache (I had my fingers crossed that the thing would work at all), then led us inside where we wrote the following chart. Andrew demanded and received from the class veto power over the suggested sentences, but in fact he didn't use it.

> Today we went outside to watch Andrew's parachute. We made a huge chalk circle and stood on it. Andrew stood in the circle. He wrapped the string around the parachute. He put his arm back and threw it as hard as he could up. And the string unwound as it floated down and the parachute opened and glided down. Gravity pulled the bolt. He threw it twice more. We came in.
>
> The end.

This story's title, "Andrew's Parachute," was dictated last, after "The end," but I was instructed to write it at the top. As you might guess, when we went for a lesson to this story the next day we did the *-ed* ending. The lesson was very gratifying. That delicious word *glided*, by the way, was a joint decision Kelly and Annie made as they watched Andrew act out how slowly

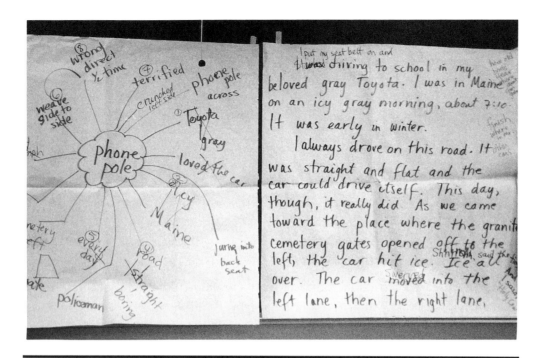

the parachute came down. Andrew's sole contribution to the story was the "gravity" sentence. It was a good adventure for all of us, and Andrew's instinct not to wait until recess was a good one.

There is no limit at all, except the ordinary limits of decency and appropriate language, to what you and the children can put on a "language experience" chart. I'm using quotation marks around the words because I don't want to limit identification of the term. What I mean by a language experience chart is any piece of text written at the dictation of the children on a chart big enough for anyone to see. The possibility for content is infinite. In earlier times, it was the custom to create "an experience" for the whole class to live through (in all senses of the term), then to direct the children to offer sequential and meaningful description of the happening. This idea was not bad, but it had the effect rather often of producing text that was the teacher's rather than the class's. I take a middle ground: what the children say I write, unless it makes no sense at all. I do it often, so that they will learn how to make more sense.

The first writing of the day, in fact, is often the News Charts, a multi-purpose five-minute adventure every morning that is part of the calendar and housekeeping chores we need to do every day. (The entry into our lives of Math Their Way has radically changed the early morning routine, and all to the good, I think, but that's another story.)

The News Charts are two pieces of chart paper hung side by side on the chalkboard or on a bulletin board if there is a wide one handy. The children come to the charts and sit for the opening exercises after the flag salute. The question I ask is, "Who has some news today about our class?" Two children talk each day, I write two sentences parallel to each other, one on each piece of chart paper. As I write each sentence, I ask for help with spelling, meaning, punctuation, and whatever else (vowels, for example, or silent letters) we are thinking of that week or day. The first thing I write, with help, is the date, and I choose a different colored marker for each chart. That way I can refer to each chart by color if I need to, and on later days by date. A child's name is almost always in the sentence, though, so we can talk about "Lisa's sentence" or "Billy's sentence." The child's name may be included and quotation marks added as in the Jeremy sentence that follows. At first, I will add them without comment, and then as one of the aspects of the sentence I "need" dictated to me.

Here are some sentences from September:

9/7	Eleven of us have kittens.	9/7	Twelve of us have dogs.
9/9	We found a tree toad at school.	9/9	Chris smiled by accident.
9/22	Jeremy says, "Perky is nice."	9/22	Two of the fish died and one is still alive.

Of course there are two sentences each day, and I have skipped a few days in this list. But the children and I are not done yet, although we have just spent five minutes talking, listening, spelling, thinking about sentence structure and the idea of what a sentence is, as well as the odd grammatical and phonetic skill, not to mention reading, since after each sentence is written I ask the whole group to read it together. Now there are two sentences, everyone knows what they say, most people have had

> **"Okay, let's count the words in Jeremy's sentence," I say.**

a little part in their construction, everyone is interested in this material—and I take full advantage of that interest and ownership to teach one of the most difficult bits of all math in the primary grades, the infamous symbols for greater than and less than, > <.

"Okay, let's count the words in Jeremy's sentence," I say. There is a murmuring pause while they each do this, and then call out their answers. Usually there is a difference of opinion, which is not at all surprising, because the act of counting without touching is a very advanced ability most of these word. When we've agreed that there are indeed five words, I write a little *5* next to the period at the end of Jeremy's sentence, and invite them to count the fish sentence, which in this case is blue. Again the divergent answers, all well within a ball park of probability, and again we count together. "Ten words," I repeat their final count, and I write a *10* next to the period at the end of the fish sentence.

"Now who can come put the thing up between them?" I ask, and choose someone who hasn't done so recently. "The thing" is a small > symbol cut out of a four-inch square of construction paper, which the chosen child places between the two sentences; I pin it there for the day. Then we read, "Jeremy's sentence is shorter than the fish sentence" or "The red sentence is shorter than the blue sentence," and then "Five is less than ten." This process is how I "teach" that "shorter" is "less," and that "less" always means the smaller number in a comparison. In just the same way we read the September 9 sentences "The green toad sentence is longer than Chris's sentence," and then "Seven is greater than four." That rather odd word "greater" begins to feel like a synonym for longer, bigger, and the other "more" words in a comparison.

I don't really think of this process as teaching, certainly not in the sense of presenting a lesson, but there sure is a lot of "drill and practice" in it, and the children never suspect that they are drilling and practicing a nearly intolerable piece of theoretical notation. It's both guided practice and independent practice, because of course this is one of the charts that children read and look at and redo with a friend or two; after a few months of this I don't have to lead them through the process, I merely scribe.

> **The children never suspect that they are drilling and practicing a nearly intolerable piece of theoretical notation.**

A day we have two equal sentences is always a very fun day, too; it happens so seldom, though, that we reinvent the equals sign in first grade. The child whose turn it is makes the two parallel "equals" lines with the marker right on the chart.

If a child has news that is very personal, such as "My Grammy is coming to see us," I often suggest that it will be good to write in the writing book about that, and ask again for "something about all of us." This distinction between class and personal news is an artificial one, to be sure, and not as cast in stone as it perhaps sounds. When we first begin this work, anything is okay. During the work of creating a chart story with a group, then, the children give their ideas and language constructions out loud to the group and the teacher, and the teacher writes them down in big print on a big sheet of paper. This format is actually the origin of the Big Book idea, one of whose premises is that the bigger the print the more accessible it is to the young eye and to the group. An instant recording of the spoken word into large print is one of the obvious benefits of this writing; the child whose sentence or idea it was can see it in print, very much in a one-to-one correspondence, which is one of those magical somethings necessary for the transformation of a nonreader into a reader.

> **When I run out of wall, I copy the charts onto dittos and keep them in a notebook and send them home as "homework" to be read to parents and other significant people in the child's life.**

I keep saying "chart" because I prefer to use big pieces of paper for small children, but the overhead works just as well for older ones. The other reason I prefer charts to acetate is that I can then mount the charts on the wall all over the room and use them for reading and for remembering until I run out of wall. Then, when I run out of wall, I copy the charts onto dittos and keep them in a notebook and send them home as "homework" to be read to parents and other significant people in the child's life.

So the day begins with a whole-group writing experience, moving almost at once into Doing Words time, where individual writing is done at several levels of development and competence. Later in the morning, after silent reading or just before lunch, depending on the idiosyncrasies of the day, we will return to the whole-group writing format, perhaps as a deliberate connection to reading.

I read Eric Carle's *The Greedy Python* at least once every year, usually fairly close to the beginning of the year. After the first page or two the children understand the rhymes in the book and begin to finish the sentences with me, calling out the rhymes. We do a little math as we go along ("'Then he ate the bat'—how many animals has he eaten now?" and so forth.) When we get to the page where he coughs up all the animals, I ask how we will have to count them as they come back out, and I get a unison shout of "Ten. Nine. . . . Blast off!" Right away we can act this episode out, choosing who will be which animal, with me, using a green sheet, being the python. We can have the animals eaten in the order they were in the book, or in order of size, or type, or alphabetically—just ask the children for more ideas. And because all the children liked that Carle story, we wrote one of the first of the many

About once a week, or perhaps three times a month, in the afternoon we will also write a chart having to do with something we are studying in the science or social studies realms.

first-grade chart stories about a python who ate, of course, many of the children, scared the rest of them, and . . .

About once a week, or perhaps three times a month, in the afternoon we will also write a chart having to do with something we are studying in the science or social studies realms.

When we begin a study of animals, for example, we talk about and find pictures of and share what we already know. Sooner or later, from our discussions and descriptions, we can begin to make generalizations and categorizations, such as animals with fur, animals with wings, animals with four legs or two, and eventually get to habitat as a classification device. The idea emerges that earth's creatures spend their time mostly in the water, on the land, or in the air, so from making lists and webs we turn to what I call a descriptive essay (dictated by the children, printed by me):

Water Animals

Water animals swim. They are fish, sharks, porcupine fish, octopuses, sunfish, lobsters, crabs, sand dollars, starfish, whales, and otters.

The blue whale is the biggest animal in the world. It's even bigger than a dinosaur.

Otters are mammals. They are hairy. They eat clams and fish. They float on their back and crack open clams on a rock on their tummies.

When we got to the sentence about the blue whale, I suggested that we read the part we'd written so far to be sure we didn't want to add anything to that part. Brandon said he knew some more about otters he wanted to add, and Aaron said he did, too. Penny said we had to do the part about whales first, and Jake agreed with her. "Whales come first, anyways," he said by way of argument, "'cause they're bigger." There was a general consensus about that, so we proceeded to do a paragraph about whales. I said, "Great, we'll do a paragraph about whales first, and then a paragraph about otters." (If I don't use the odd words like *paragraphing* in their context from time to time, no one will have ever heard of them when an appropriate moment comes to make something of them! Children and other humans can live perfectly contented lives without ever paragraphing anything, you know. It's not a natural skill.)

As it turned out, the information about whales was, to my mind, rather sparse. I think myself one of the most interesting things about whales is that they sing, but the size factor was the important one for this group. The connection of dinosaurs to whales (or nearly anything, for that matter) with six-year-olds is sure-fire, and I know these children had seen on television the amazing clam-cracking that otters do on their tummies. When I asked what else the children wanted to say about otters, they had nothing more to add. So we read the whole thing and hung it up to admire until the next day.

Part of our task the next day was to read a chart together, and I told them I wanted to read that one to be sure we remembered it. "O' course we do," said Chris scornfully. "We wrote it, didn't we?" I was gratified to find that my role as invisible recorder had worked once more.

They stayed in their seats for this one, and I retrieved the chart from its piece of wall and plastered it temporarily to the chalkboard with tape.

"Shall we read it all together?" I invited, and we began. It always surprises me how willing young children are to read together, even those who are really not able to read the material alone. It's a walking, talking support group, I know, but it is always a surprise to me. When we finished the choral reading I asked

> **"Let's look at those names for a minute. Spell yours for me, Nick," and I wrote on the board the letters he said, and did the same for Mindy.**

who could read the title. A zillion hands went up, and I chose Ellen, who is so quiet I miss her too often. (She was on my list of people-to-watch-out-for that day.) Ellen dutifully read the title and stopped, which told me that she knew what titles are.

"Now you choose someone to read the next sentence," I told her, which I knew was much harder for this retiring little someone than reading; she managed to do it, though, choosing Mindy. Mindy chose Aaron, Aaron chose Nick, and so on until the whole essay was read, sentence by sentence.

"So," I said in a contemplative voice, "we had Mindy and Nick read today, among others. Let's look at those names for a minute. Spell yours for me, Nick," and I wrote on the board the letters he said, and did the same for Mindy. "Nick. Mindy," I said slowly. "What letter have they both got?" Concentration by the group for a second or two, then calls of "*i*" and "*n*" came out of the group. "Right," I said. "Good observing," I remembered to say. "Let's look at the *i* today, the vowel in these names," I directed blatantly. I circled the *i* in both the names on the board. "What does that *i* say? What sound does that vowel *i* make in *Nick* and in *Mindy*?"

This phonics lesson lasted about ten minutes, and I followed it up later by reading aloud after lunch as usual and stopping when I heard a particularly good example of the short-*i* sound.

A little longer concentration and some drawn out murmuring of the two names. I waited a long minute. "What do you think?" I asked. "Got a sound in your mouth?" Some nods. "Okay, let's hear it when my hand comes down to my side." I raised my arm and then dropped it, and a chorus of short-i sounds came stuttering at me. "Terrific!" I beamed. "Good sounding! Now, . . . "

"Okay, we can find them in the chart," interrupted Nick. "I see one! I'll do it!"

We had done this "find the sound" game on every chart since the first one on the first day of school, beginning of course with the easiest consonants, and now we were beginning to find the short *i*. As it turned out there were only four *is* in the Water Animals story that weren't short *i*, so there was a lot of reinforcement. Each student who volunteered to find one had to read it, or ask us all to read it together, so we could all be sure. Then the finder got to circle the *i* with a marker and choose the next finder. *Their* and *hairy* were the hardest ones—*porcupine* was obviously not the same as *Nick*, and *tummies* had a silent one, they decided. I didn't choose to go into the problem of whether in fact it is the *i* or the *e* that is silent in *tummies*, since we were chasing after the short-*i* sound this time.

This phonics lesson lasted about ten minutes, and I followed it up later by reading aloud after lunch as usual and stopping when I heard a particularly good example of the short-*i* sound. Later that week we used this chart again as a review of the plural -*s* with enormous success. These children were old hands at plural -*s* by this time. Before we were done with this study of animals, we had charts of Land Animals and Flying Animals and Camouflage, too, done the same way. We reviewed short *a* in the Land chart, and found a couple of examples of -*ing* in the other ones.

After we've done this examination of our own texts a few times, I think it's legitimate to begin to ask students to spell the short-*i* words, for example, in a chart as we are writing one together, that is as I am recording what they are composing orally. The point of phonics, after all, is to be able to make reasonable guesses about spelling as you are writing; this is exactly what I am trying to model, always using the children's own text, in this case a group text, as the vehicle.

So we do news in the language experience format; we do small science essays and reports; we do extended, true-to-life experience stories, such as "How We Made Mud," or "Our Trip to the Planetarium," which are as time honored as anything is in grammar school; not least we write fictional and fantastical stuff. We do once-in-a-lifetime moments, too, such as Andrew's parachute.

Occasionally we write a fictional piece together, but not often, because the children are usually deep into their own fictional writings. It is a good way to model the parts of a story, though, so occasionally we do it. This time is another opportunity for me to mention such literary understandings as *beginning, setting, characters, development, title, ending, and plot.* One typical piece of fiction, with only the most rudimentary development, is called "The Bell," and was written, as you will instantly perceive, at the end of October.

The Bell

Once upon a time there was a church that had a bell. The churchyard was haunted. Spiders were in spider webs in the belfry. Kellie and Tiffany and Brooke went to look at the church. They snuck out at midnight. The door squeaked. There were bats fluttering in the belfry. They heard ghosts howling. Witches were laughing.

They heard the church bell ring 12 times.

A bat chased them and they all ran home.

The beginning, middle, and ending of stories are best taught by exposing students to them. Read enough good stories and talk about the b, m, and e, and children will know which part is which and how odd it is when one is missing. In this story the beginning was two-fold: the o.u.a.t. standby and a clear description of setting. The energy of this writing, though, was in the middle. As they were talking about this story, I said, "Let's be sure to have a lot going on in the middle of this story," and lo! look at all those wonderful verbs going on! All the energy was used up by the time the children had done those middle sentences—interestingly this was mostly the work of the girls in the class—so the ending is abrupt and anticlimactic. The children in the story were working through some Halloween fears, I think, and they wanted to get home fast! "Lots of noises here," I commented when we were reading it aloud together. So various children took the marker and circled the ten words we could all agree were sound words. Alan wanted to have twelve rings in the list because it rang twelve times, but he was dissuaded, not to say squashed, by Brooke.

With every passing day, sophistication in story-writing grows. After six months or so of daily writing on individual stories, hearing many stories read, writing some together as well, and reading others during individual reading time, children in the primary grades have an ever-clearer picture of what makes a story work. I hear them talking to each other in conference about whether an ending is abrupt, "happens too fast"; whether there is enough detail; why some part is confusing because it's not connected to what goes before it. An example of how these concerns come into play in a chart story is in the chapter story we did when the whole school was involved in a study of the Middle Ages.

Once there was a knight named Aaron who had a squire named Michael. Aaron was wearing armor on his back and his chest and his arms and his legs. On his head was helmet. Michael was wearing a leather tunic and a red cape. Michael had a sword and Aaron had a lance. They met up with a fierce scaly dragon. Aaron stabbed the dragon in the stomach with his lance. The dragon roared. "I'm hungry!"

So Aaron pulled out his lance and Michael stabbed his sword in the dragon's heart. Then he died.

They rode back to the castle and got 50 guards. They pulled the dragon to the castle with ropes tied to its body. They shoved it into a huge oven—they scraped the scales off first—and cooked it 18 hours.

When we read this story a day or two later we had a full-class conference about it, too. Everybody liked it all, of course, especially the parts with lances and swords, but there were a few questions.

"What did they do with it then?" Mindy wanted to know.

"They fed it to the dogs, I bet," said Chris. "I bet dragons taste awful!"

"No," said John positively. "They were all really poor then you know, except the knights, so the villagers would've split it up and eaten it all." He paused a minute and tilted his head consideringly at Chris. "But I bet they gave the bones to the dogs!"

"Shall I add something here, then?" I asked.

"Better put in that they all ate the dragon," decided Aaron. Various approving sounds.

"What shall I say? Who has a sentence?"

"Put 'They fed it to the whole village,'" commanded Rachel G. "Then we don't have to have a separate sentence about the dogs."

So that sentence was added to the end of the story.

"I have a question," I said. They looked at me, curious but not surprised. "See up here on the second page where Michael stabs him? Where it says 'Then he died?' My question is, Who died? It sounds like Michael did."

"No, no," came various voices, "it was the dragon who died!"

"Well, I know that," I said patiently, "but the way it's written there it sounds like it's Michael."

"Hold it," said Michael, surging to his feet and moving toward the chart. "Let me read this thing." I had my hand on the chart where the odd sentence was, but he found it easily by looking for his own name. "'Michael stabbed his sword in the dragon's heart,'" he read. "'Then he died.' Hmmm. Well, I'll tell you, I know I didn't die and the dragon did, and if everybody else doesn't know I'm still alive we'd better *do* something!"

He sat down to admiring laughter. I took up my marker.

"How shall we revise this to make that clearer?" I asked.

"Better just say it, just plain," advised Anne. "'Then the dragon died.'"

So we did.

This story hung for two more days before someone realized it had no title. Several titles were suggested, such as "Aaron's Dragon Hunt" (guess whose idea that was) and "Cooking at the Castle" (mine); the group finally voted, and on the third ballot the title was "The Knight, the Squire, and the Dragon." We later used the story for more practice with the *-ed* ending, having a very interesting time with *fed*.

Even more directive, though, but lots of fun, is a story such as the one we wrote a few years ago called "Two Astronauts," or, as it was originally transcribed, "two astronaut."

This story was an interesting review, too, of how much the children had learned about space travel, but its main purpose was to be a sampler of errors the children could edit for in their own work. As they made up the story, I used a different color marker for each speaker, which effectively worked out to a different color for each sentence. That way they could tell me that the problem was "in the blue sentence," for example. The story looked like this to begin with:

two astronaut

once a pon a tim there wus a astronaut named RacheL And anotheR astronaut nameD Andrew they were on their way To Uranus then They crashd inTo a asteroid The spacecraft was Hideouslee damaged, The nose cone was crushed And the engine's oxygen leaked out into spac Andrew and Rachel almost died they fixed the Radio and called base. Another ship came and rescued Them

What a mess, eh? The children who were sharpest in language began to notice my mistakes at about the second sentence. "Hey, you're doing that all wrong!" was Anne's succinct observation. I merely smiled and said, "So then what happened?" and we went on. It was a very lot of fun to find all the mistakes, too, and believe it or not they found them all, except for *Hideouslee*.

I was very proud of them, and said so.

The possibilities are almost infinite. Another chart I often do is the outline chart, which I use for reports in a particular area of study, such as the space study we usually do in January.

In January not much in the animal and vegetable worlds is going on, but the incredible universe is always around us. Every year, when we first start to study the solar system, we look at photographs and models and maps of the moon and write about it, with some subtle guidance, on a chart. When we are finished the chart can stand as a model for the reports the students will be doing on the planetary body of their choice as the concluding writing of the study. After we talk about the moon, which still fascinates children even though there are some footprints and tire tracks on it now, we write a chart about it and then begin to talk about the planets. It's certainly possible to write a piece, too, about any or all of the planets, certainly even more possible now that *Voyager* has passed them all than it was when I first began teaching, but by January I think they can write their own pieces. The planets chart, then, is an outline of what will be in their reports:

Tell what it looks like.

Tell the name of the planet.

Tell if it has life or air or water.

Describe its atmosphere.

Tell how many moons it has.

Tell how big it is.

Tell how far away it is.

Tell one special thing.

This pattern, which we develop in answer to the question "What would a reader want to know about 'your' planet?" is helpful for the duration of the planet study, and if we forgot anything we can always revise the chart. Some years I write the parts of this list in different colors so if Douglas gets stuck I can say, "Read me the red sentence." "Tell how many moons it has." "Have you told that yet?" "No." "Can you tell that next?" "Okay."

> **Since I hadn't lived with the students every day of the year, I didn't know what they knew, so we did a webbing first.**

I did this same thing the other day with some second graders, only about animals instead of planets. Since I hadn't lived with the students every day of the year, I didn't know what they knew, so we did a webbing first. On the web appeared such things as *fur, feathers, den, ocean, eggs, mammals, eat meat, four legs, habitat*. So the list of what-to-include-in-your-report was the following:

Tell its name.

Tell what it looks like, how many legs, and what covers it.

Tell its habitat and where it lives.

Tell what kind of animals.

Tell what it eats.

Tell what is special about it and why you chose it.

The words in the webbing served, too, as a kind of instant dictionary for the children as this work progressed.

Another way to own and use language is to do what are currently known as "innovations." (An innovation carried by a high school student to its full extension could be called plagiarism, but I prefer to think of such innovations as flattery.) An innovation is a reworking, a rewriting of a story or poem or song so that the children are stretching their understanding of a form, or an element of English, or their understanding of a technique of writing. Another way to talk about this stretching is to say that children take what has meaning for them in a story or poem or song and make it their own, or that they insert themselves into the form established by the story or poem or song.

The song "Sally Go 'Round the Sun" has a simple form that can be changed by changing the final noun, by changing the initial name, or by changing the preposition. After they learn the original song, the children can do innovations orally or on sentence strips.

The original follows:

> Sally go 'round the sun,
>
> Sally go 'round the moon,
>
> Sally go 'round the sunshine,
>
> Every afternoon.

It becomes, after a discussion of what other things Sally could go around, the following:

> Sally go 'round the flagpole,
>
> Sally go 'round the jungle gym,
>
> Sally go 'round the swing set,
>
> Every afternoon.

When the song is really familiar, change several parts:

> Katie go 'round the chair,
>
> Marcus go under the bed,
>
> Ian go through the window,
>
> Every afternoon.

Taking a whole book, such as Eric Carle's *The Grouchy Ladybug* in the primary grades, is more of a challenge. As we are reading it (several times), the children become adept at filling in the repetitive parts if I break off.

"Hey, you," I read, then look at the children, who respond chorally with the next line of the book. "Want to fight?" Then we talk about other bugs or animals which they might meet and challenge, and the children work in pairs to create a new part based on the rhythm of the original, then illustrate it. We can bind such a collection as our own "Grouchy _____" book.

Another kind of innovation occurs when the students take the central idea of a story and relate it to an emotion they have all experienced.

There are many books in the primary repertoire that lend themselves to this kind of vocabulary, classification, and phonics innovation. *It Looked Like Spilt Milk* and *In a Dark, Dark Wood* are two commonly used.

Another kind of innovation occurs when the students take the central idea of a story and relate it to an emotion they have all experienced. When I read *Franklin in the Dark*, after students filling in the endings of the repeating phrases chorally, we list all the animals and what they were afraid of; then we list "all the things Franklin is afraid of," discovering that, in fact, there is only one thing. Then we list all the many, many things Franklin is not afraid of, from heights to walking by himself. Then I ask the children to tell what they are not afraid of, from monsters to Mom (although I draw the line at Ninja Turtle characters), and we make a book of all these. This activity makes a class book, or, if I xerox everyone's pages, an individual book for each child of all the things we all aren't afraid of, to take home and read. *The Maybe Garden* and *The Runaway Bunny* can also be used in this way.

Remembering every minute the child-centered nature of our work, we see that language experience is quintessentially child centered. Next to key Words, which are the child's individual concerns and captions, language experience charts are almost the definition of *child centered*. The work with charts in the classroom is different only in that it is not individual. Experiencing language is the way to learn and own it.

Notes: Chart Stories

Some advantages of large groups are:

- Everyone has the same experiences.
- Everyone has contributed and so has some ownership.
- Possibilities for language are limitless.

Rules of thumb for doing chart stories:

- Never use yellow markers, which are visible only from two millimeters away!
- Ask questions of the children who know the answer (Kelli for the quotation marks, Joey for the beginning sound).
- Ask for help with something in each sentence ("Who can tell me what *bear* starts with?").
- Read the chart together after every few sentences.
- Generally, figure out the title last.
- Go over the chart again with some element in mind (a sound, a kind of word, such as hearing or moving, an inflection such as 's), and have the children take turns highlighting, by circling or otherwise marking, that element.
- Four or five sentences or ideas are enough for five-year-olds.

- Fill the chart with text with children from age six to nine

  as an opportunity to model the creation of text

  as an opportunity to highlight an element of phonics or language or writing

  as an opportunity to practice reading aloud

Copy the chart onto a sheet of ordinary paper to use

- as seatwork or review, to highlight the same element
- as homework, to read at home and highlight the element

Do innovations with a book or a song, making its rhythm and plan part of the child's own repertoire. Here are a few strong possibilities:

- *It Looked Like Spilt Milk*
- *The Grouchy Ladybug*
- *In a Dark, Dark Wood*
- *Harry and the Terrible Whatzit*
- *Franklin in the Dark*
- *The Maybe Garden*
- *The Runaway Bunny*

4

Literature Brings Characters and Settings to Life

"I went to a bookstore yesterday after school," I told the second-grade class as they settled down on the rug in front of me, ready for the after-recess reading.

"And you bought *another* new book for us," finished Tiffany, beaming. This was the third or fourth time I'd taken over for this class's teacher, who was having a difficult pregnancy.

"Well, I bought another new book for me, Tiffany," I beamed back, "but I want to read it to you, too. Here it is."

I held up *Friday Night Is Papa Night*. "This is called *Friday Night Is Papa Night*," I said, running my right hand under the title as I spoke it. "And it says," I turned the book around so it was facing me "it was written by Ruth A. Sonneborn with pictures by Emily A. McCully," I said slowly. I turned it around and pointed to the printed words that said that. "So Ruth Sonneborn is the . . . "

"Author!" called out several children.

"And Emily McCully is the . . . "

"Illustrator," came the answer.

"Right," I agreed. "Does anyone know another book by these people?"

Various versions of "no" and "I don't" floated out of the group, and I shook my head, too. "I think I've read something else by this writer, but I can't think what it is, either." I raised my eyebrows at them. "When you go to the library next time, maybe you can ask Mrs. Reynolds if she knows of any more books by Ruth Sonneborn."

James was holding his hand up straight and still, unwilling to simply speak into silence, so I said his name.

"I know this book," he said. "I have it, but it has a different cover."

"So you've read it?" I asked.

James nodded.

"Great," I said. "Did you like it? Shall I go ahead and read it?" I was clutching the book to my chest now, concentrating on James.

"Yes," replied James, ever correct in his speech. That was all, so I assumed it meant yes to both questions.

"Thanks, James," I said, and showed the group the book again. They were all settled now, feet crossed. "Let's all read the title," I invited them, and read it slowly myself with some accompanying and some echoing voices joining me. "What do you think it will be about?"

> **"Let's all read the title," I invited them, and read it slowly myself with some accompanying and some echoing voices joining me. "What do you think it will be about?"**

A little silence while the children looked at the picture on the cover, which shows a little boy standing at the top of a set of stairs at the door of his house, with three other children looking out from a window to the left of that door. All the children are looking anxious or sad, all have black hair and brownish skins. The boy by the door is wearing yellow pajamas.

"There are some kids in it," offered Justine, pointing at the book.

"Four," agreed James efficiently.

"What is he wearing?" exclaimed Kellie, giggling behind her hand. "It looks like he's wearing his pajamas!"

She raised a giggle from Alison, but that was all. The others were concentrating on the cover.

"I think they're in a city," said Marc. "That looks like a apartment building, like in a city."

"Why are they all so sad?" asked Maria. "Did their Papa die?"

"Yeah, what's the matter?" several others asked.

"You'd better read it, teacher," said Samuel resignedly.

So I read the book, page by page, picture by picture, and all of the children were anxious, too, in the middle, and finally as happy as Pedro of the yellow pajamas was at the end.

"Who can tell me a part they liked best about this story?" I asked after we had all digested the story a little. I looked around for a face that was considering the question. "Amanda?" I tilted my head at her.

"I liked it all, but I liked it when he woke up in the middle of the night. That's scary. I bet he was scared, too."

I turned to the page that showed, against a dark background, Pedro's face and his hands holding the bed covers up to his chin.

"How do you know Pedro's scared? How does the illustrator let you know that in her picture?" I held that picture up for them all to see.

"You can tell by his face," said Tisha, with some impatience. "He *looks* scared!"

"His eyes are real big," added Marc. "Like this!" And he made a scared face with wide, wide eyes, cowering back with his hands raised.

Some of his friends laughed appreciatively. "That's it, Marc," I agreed. "You could've been the model." I paused, holding the picture out. "Anything else scary about this picture?"

"He's covering up his pajamas," said Tiffany, positively. "That makes it scary too."

"It's a scary picture because his pajamas are under the covers?" I repeated, at a loss myself about why that was scary. I waited, but Tiffany didn't seem as puzzled as I. "Because he wants to cover up as much as he can?" I guessed.

Light dawned on me. It was the color that made it scarier. "If the illustrator had let his yellow pajamas show it wouldn't have been as dark," I rephrased, finally catching on.

"Well, yes, and besides it makes it all black, like, dark." I was still looking at her, so she got up and took the book, turning the pages. She found the one before and showed it. "There, see? The yellow is under the covers."

Light dawned on me. It was the color that made it scarier. "If the illustrator had let his yellow pajamas show it wouldn't have been as dark," I rephrased, finally catching on.

Tiffany nodded. Bert said, "Oh," in a gently discovering tone. He was the true artist in the group—I was surprised he hadn't had Tiffany's idea.

"The illustrator shows us that he's scared by showing us his face a certain way and certain things in certain colors," I summed up. "So how does the author let us know that Pedro is scared?" A short pause. "Shall I read it again?" Lots of nods.

"'Suddenly Pedro awoke. He opened his eyes. The kitchen was very dark and empty. There was just one spot of light on the floor by the window. Pedro sat up in bed. And then he remembered. Papa. Papa had not come home. There on the kitchen table was Papa's plate, his fork, his knife, his spoon, his glass, his napkin—still on the table. All clean and unused.'" I turned the page. "'Pedro got out of bed and ran to the window. He looked down into the street. A noisy car drove by. Two people walked past. Where was Papa? Why hadn't he come home?'"

I closed the book without showing the pictures. "How does the author, Ruth Sonneborn, tell you how he feels? Did she say, 'Pedro was scared'? Did anybody hear that word?"

"No," came several voices, then Alex's. "You know, I don't think he was so much scared. I think he was worried about his dad."

"Now there's a new word," I said. "I'd better write these words down." I moved nearer to the chart stand and on a blank sheet wrote *Pedro* on one side with a line under it, and under the line I wrote *scared* and *worried* in a list. "How does the author tell you Pedro's worried, Alex?" I asked, turning back from writing.

"'Cause he's looking out the window and, you know, wondering where he is, he says 'Where is he?' I think he's worried lots of times in this book. Remember where they're eating and he doesn't want to? Read that part again."

I turned to the page he meant.

"'The children came to the table. No one talked. Then Pedro said, "I don't want any supper. I want Papa." He began to cry.'"

"Do those words show you that he was worried?" I asked.

Alex nodded. "What does the illustrator show?" asked Bert.

I showed the picture. Several children moved closer to see better.

"Yep," said Jack. "That's a worried face if I ever saw one."

"Let's vote," I said. Kids love to vote.

James raised his hand, carefully as always. "There is something that both the author and the illustrator do that I don't get," he said clearly. "Why is his bed in the kitchen?"

"Interesting question," I replied. "Why is his bed in the kitchen? Why would people have one kid's bed in the kitchen?"

Several children spoke at once. "Wait a minute, wait a minute," I said, holding up my hands in mock horror. "What a garble! One at a time, please."

Jack, immediately: "They don't have enough bedrooms!"

Tiffany, with her hand up, too: "At my aunt's house my aunt and uncle sleep on the couch every night. And turn it into a couch in the day."

Kellie, ever judgmental: "That's weird."

"You have enough bedrooms for everybody at your house," I said to Kellie. She nodded. I looked around at them all. "Do you think there are enough bedrooms for everybody at Pedro's house?" Various responses blew around. "Let's vote," I said. Kids love to vote. "Who thinks there are?" A few hands, which we counted out loud. "Who thinks there aren't?" Many hands, which we counted. "Well, that's a decisive vote," I reported. "Now why is that so, do you think? Why don't they get a bigger apartment, so everyone would fit?"

"Probably they don't have enough money," said Marc.

"They're too poor," said James succinctly.

"Does Ruth Sonneborn tell us that, just plain, or does she show us with other words?"

"She shows us." I added *poor* to the list.

"And they didn't have enough money for a telephone, either, remember?" added Alex.

"Oh yeah," answered Sara, "that's another thing."

> **"Great," I said. "You are all really good at seeing how the author shows you how people feel without telling you."**

"Great," I said. "You are all really good at seeing how the author shows you how people feel without telling you. Let me read one more part, now, and see if you know what she's showing here:

"'He hurried across the kitchen and turned on the light. The kitchen now looked brighter than day. He ran to the door and opened it wide. "Papa!" Pedro shouted. "Papa, you're here." He hugged Papa and Papa hugged him.'"

I closed the book. "How does Pedro feel now?"

"Happy," came the unanimous answer. Jerome, who hadn't spoken before, stood up in the middle of the group. "That boy is *happy*," he said, with heavy emphasis in his voice and a "Yeah!" upward motion of his fist. "His daddy is come *home!*"

"You are *right*, Jerome," I answered, grinning, imitating his hand motion. "Yeah!"

Everybody laughed and "Yeah!" repeated all over. I wrote *happy* on the list.

"Now look at this list," I said, "here are four things we know about Pedro and Ruth Sonneborn never uses any of these words to tell us. She lets us make up our own minds because of the words she uses. That's what writers do—use their words to make pictures and ideas in our heads. She shows us instead of telling us how they feel."

Tiffany raised her hand. "You know, teacher, we could make another list there for the other people, like his sister. She was real nice but the author didn't say that, either."

"You never heard the word *nice* but you know that sister was nice, don't you? Is this Ruth Sonneborn a good writer?"

"Yeah!" came the response. "She makes pictures with words the way the illustrator makes pictures with paint," elaborated the usually monosyllabic Bert. I couldn't have said it better myself.

"Exactly," I replied. "Just . . . like . . . you . . . writers . . . do, . . . too," I said slowly, pointing at various ones as I spoke. "Just like you."

I let this sink in, while I put up another piece of large paper next to the list we'd agreed on. "Let's practice this just once," I said. "Look at these words now—can we read them together?"

Chorus of "scared, worried, poor, happy."

"Who thinks they could show us one of these words, act it out in the circle here?"

After a minute Janetta raised her hand. "I can," she said, and stood up.

"Great," I said. "Can the rest of you move a little, please, so Janetta has room?" A lot of scooting followed, but they organized themselves fairly quickly. Jack took the opportunity to shove hard against Jerome, so I stood up and reached over toward him. "You come here and sit with me, Jack," which he did. I gave him my markers to hold.

Janetta was standing in the middle of the group, posing. "Wow, nice showing!" I said. "What's the word she's showing?"

"Scared!" came the chorus.

"Right," said Janetta, breaking the pose and going toward her place.

"No, no, stay there please Janetta," I said. "Let's put what she's showing us into words, let's write a picture of her being scared. Do it again, please." Janetta took up her pose again. "Now what's she doing?" I asked, uncapping a marker and giving the cap back to Jack.

"She's got her hands up over her eyes," said Tiffany.

"'Janetta has her hands up over her eyes,'" I wrote, saying the words as I did so. "Can she see through them?"

"She's peeking through her fingers," said Alison.

"'She's peeking through her fingers,'" I wrote.

Silence.

"What's the rest of her body like?" I asked.

"It's all twisted and like bent away," said Jack.

"Boy," I said, looking at Janetta. "It sure is! How can I write that?"

"Her body's all twisted and bent away from something she's looking at," Marc instructed me. I wrote that down. "Anything else? Should I write that she's looking at something?"

"You just did," said James.

"Right," I agreed. "What else, then? What about her eyes, or her mouth? Is she saying anything or making any noise?"

"Eeek," squealed Janetta obligingly. Lots of laughs rewarded her.

"Write 'she said eeek,'" commanded Sal.

I wrote. I was almost at the bottom of the chart, so I put a line a little way under the writing.

"There. Thanks, Janetta. Great acting, great showing with words." I clapped, and the others joined as she sat down. "Now let's all read it."

We read the whole chart together chorally, in our usual fashion, with Brent and Jerome a heartbeat behind everyone, Marc and Alex a heartbeat ahead.

"Now you can do this, too," I said, "just like all writers do, when you write a story. If someone in it is scared, or happy, or worried, you can show your readers, don't just tell them." I put the date on the chart and capped the marker. Just then—and I hadn't arranged this—the door opened and a sixth-grader came in with a message for me.

"Thanks," I said. Suddenly I had an idea. "Oh! Say, have you got a minute? Can you guess something for us?"

The sixth-grader shuffled his feet the way they do and tried not to smile. "SureIguessso," he shrugged with voice and shoulders. I turned to the class and quickly flipped the Pedro list over so he couldn't see it. With a loud stage-whisper I said, "Let's test this writing we did. See if he can guess what word this shows, shall we?"

> **"Now you can do this, too," I said, "just like all writers do, when you write a story. If someone in it is scared, or happy, or worried, you can show your readers, don't just tell them."**

Lots of nods, smiles, enthusiasm, and we read the whole paragraph again. When we finished everyone looked at the big kid.

"So in one word, how would you say this kid in the writing feels?" I asked in my friendliest way.

"Well . . . I'd say scared," said the sixth-grader, shifting his feet again.

Spontaneous applause, cheers, and more "Yeah!" fist movements rewarded him. I clapped too. "Thanks a lot!" I said. Then I wrote *scared*, in a different color, on the line at the bottom.

"Welcome," said the big kid, really almost letting himself smile.

"'Bye Jason," said a few brave voices from the rug as he went out.

"Okay, children, it's time to get ready for lunch now. Show me a terrific line today, please." And as they scrambled toward their lunch boxes and coats Bert lagged behind, his eyes twinkling.

"We'll show you, but we won't tell you," he said.

Now of course not every child will immediately transfer this "showing" of characterization to her writing. I have done this lesson with children from grade one through grade eight, and I don't think any of them immediately internalized this way of describing the feelings of their characters. Nor can I claim that never again did a young writer write about a friend with the penultimate sentence, "Jessica (or whoever) is nice." The device of "showing, not telling" is, however, an essential one for good writers, and there is no reason why children can't do it, too.

To my mind, this kind of description is particularly valuable in our television times. With the visual overload television brings, there is never enough opportunity to hear descriptive language and to find how words can make pictures in our minds. I use a well-written book, even a short one, to show young writers how their language can do just that.

Showing-not-telling, also known as descriptive writing, isn't limited to characterization. Setting is equally important in all writing, and one way to highlight it, also, is to read a piece of "real" writing, such as the first ten or twelve lines of chapter 4 of *Charlotte's Web,* a lovely and easily pictured setting. (By the way, E. B. White's *Charlotte's Web* is just about all you'd ever need to teach just about anything you'd ever want or need to teach about writing, anytime. It has the added advantage of being known by nearly every American child, too, which familiarity makes its use as a teaching tool much less scary to both teachers and students of all ages.)

Whenever I read this bit of *Charlotte,* I read it twice, slowly. Then I ask all the listeners to "draw the setting"—and if that direction requires that we define setting, we do it then and there—on a sheet of plain old ditto paper, 8½ by 11 inches, with a pencil or a pen. They can draw the setting on notebook paper, too, but it's not as pretty. After about five minutes, during which time I peer over a few shoulders and say "Mmmm" admiringly, I start to draw the setting myself on the chalkboard, as quietly as possible. About now there may be a provocative boy or two choosing to make raindrops with loud tappings of their pencils. Usually I ignore this; if I'm interrupted myself, I grab a magazine and slip one under that boy's drawing, not saying a word.

> **Using real books to teach writing, using real books to teach reading—what could be more organic than that?**

When we are all done, we talk. I read back over the selection, and tell the children to put a plus sign at the top of their pictures if they included each of the things in it. It's merely a way to bring closure to the event, and older children like to think, because they've been trained to, that I am evaluating or "checking" their work.

The connection here between a "real" book and the work that writers do is very clear. Using real books to teach writing, using real books to teach reading—what could be more organic than that?

Notes: Literature for Learning

Drawing believable characters is an important skill for writers, young or old. *Friday Night is Papa Night* is a whole book to read, listening and looking for ways the author is showing, not telling, what the book's characters are like. Robert Munsch's *The Paper Bag Princess* is another one that works very well, especially with children in grades above second grade. Read the book sometime, not the same day you will do the characterization lesson, so that the children know the story.

For the characterization lesson

- Begin by reminding the children of the story and list the characters in columns on the board (or chart or overhead).

- Read the story, and after each part ask the children to say how each character feels now.

- Write the adjective the children give under the name of the character.

- Read all the lists ("at times the dragon was mean, and vain, and full, and tired").

- Have one child demonstrate one word.

- Tell the children to put themselves in groups of three, with one actor, one writer, and one idea person.

- Ask them to choose one of the words on the lists, act it out, write a sentence about what the actor's face looks like, what the actor's body looks like, and what the actor's voice is doing without using the word they chose.

- Share in groups, have the other children guess, clap.

- Look at the books you like to read to your class. Quote the "showing" parts and ask them to draw the scene.

For the setting lesson

- Read the passage (not more than a paragraph).

- Ask the children for a few things they remember.

- Read the passage again.

- Ask the students to draw everything they can remember about this setting.

- Draw too.

- Read it again, slowly, stopping at each detail; have them put tiny pluses at the top of their papers if they included that detail.

5

Connecting with Sign

Buddy was a small, tired, scrappy six-year-old. He was pretty much always hungry, had a charming smile that he didn't yet realize the power of, and tended to be suspicious of kindness. Buddy's house was notorious in the town for wild parties, arrests for various kinds of brawling, and the convinced opinion of the suspicious that any and all kinds of drugs could be had there. Not only had I never met his parents, I never met any of his adult relatives, although the school was populated with many of his cousins. None of them were intellectual world-beaters, but the charming smile reappeared.

Not surprisingly, Buddy didn't have much inclination for learning. In addition—I think—he had difficulty relating sounds and symbols, so that even when he was interested and curious, the world of print made very little sense to him. He did just fine with song, memorizing the words and putting the tunes into his voice, or vice versa, just fine.

But reading was a disaster. I was discouraged, too.

Somewhere during the late fall of Buddy's year in first grade, I took an adult education night school class in beginning sign language on Thursday nights, and I zipped into class every Friday with new signs to show the kids, new ways to "talk." Eventually we all learned the manual alphabet, and everyone in the class learned to fingerspell his or her name. Jon and Kelly, the leading lights of that class, learned everyone's name, of course; even Buddy learned the four hand movements for his own name.

I began to branch out and to put signs with the songs we learned, as much as was practical, at least. The first song I put signs to is a little thing about colors, the refrain of a longer song:

> Red and yellow and pink and green,
> Purple and orange and blue.
>
> (*chorus*)
> I can sing a rainbow, sing a rainbow, sing a rainbow too.

The signs for the colors red, yellow, purple, green, pink, and blue are the letters *r, y, p, g, p,* and *b* made in the air in certain ways. We sang and signed this song for several days and found ourselves humming it at odd moments, lining up with it ("When we sing the color of your shirt, line up for lunch"), and so on. The next week it happened that I learned the sign for *ready*, which also involves the sign for *r*, and Amanda exclaimed out loud, "Oh! It's just like *red*!"

We were in the circle just then. Every morning after writing time, all of us, the children and I, gathered in a circle to read our writings to each other before recess. Ben had just finished reading his story, about dinosaurs, and had gotten sidetracked into that eternal question, Is it okay to call Apatosaurus Brontosaurus? The concentration of the group was disintegrating, so I entered in.

"Thanks, Ben," I said. "May I have everybody's attention, now, since we've all read?" The dinosaur discussion tapered off.

"Ready, class?" I pulled them together. "Ready?" and I signed the ready sign twice. Into the resulting silence came Amanda's exclamation. Signing produces an amazing silence among hearing primary children, so everybody heard Amanda's discovery.

Now you have to understand that Buddy was very keen on Amanda, and paid very close attention to her at all times. I sometimes felt he was panting, but Amanda didn't mind. So when she made her discovery about *red* and *ready*, Buddy noticed.

While Buddy was staring at her, listening intently, I said, "Yes, they are made with the same letter-sign, aren't they?"

Rachel immediately added, with some indignation, "That's in my name!" She fingerspelled *r, a, c, h, e, l,* pretty fast, too, and looked at the others. "See? That's *r*, too, at the beginning of *Rachel*."

"And at the beginning of *red* and *ready*, too," said Amanda, taking firm hold of her discovery again.

Buddy was watching Amanda, making the *r* with his fingers just as she did. Then he pointed his *r* fingers at Rachel. "Your name starts this way, too?" he checked.

"Of course!" sputtered Rachel." *R* is for Rachel. Just like *B* is for *Buddy*, you know." Sarcasm, but Buddy didn't hear it and I ignored it.

"Oh!" said Amanda again. She looked up at Buddy. "Look!" she bounced. She began singing and signing the color song, and others joined her. When she got to *blue*, she stopped, waving her hand—the blue sign is kind of a wave—at Buddy. "Look at that!" she urged him.

He looked at that, made a *b* himself, and then smiled his wonderful smile of understanding (or it might have been love) at Amanda. "Hey, that's what starts my name too, that's what starts *Buddy*. B starts *blue* and *Buddy*!"

Well, well, I thought, also entranced. I think he's got it.

About three years later Jacky came to first grade. He was almost a clone of Buddy in many ways: Jacky was small for his age, which was six, was tired all the time, always ate every scrap of school lunch, no matter what it was. Jacky, too, was a July birthday. Boys with July and August birthdays seem less likely to have all the maturity they need to acquire language even if all other elements of their lives are stable; Buddy's and Jacky's lives were not stable.

Jacky's mother ruled with an iron hand; she told me so herself. "If a kid doesn't behave you just gotta smack 'em," she said one September afternoon, her face as grim and determined as her words. "Right here and now I give you full permission to smack Jacky every time he needs it," she gestured, just missing Jacky, who was clinging to her pocketbook. His younger brother was hanging on Mom's other side; the sister kept still in her arms.

Every time he does? I thought. No "if he does" about it, eh? Expect the worst and guess what will happen, I answered her in my head while I made politer noises with my mouth.

By this time in my development as a teacher, sign language was a definite part of my repertoire, and Jacky's class routinely learned to sign "thank you," "may I go to the bathroom," "ready," "later," the colors and the numbers, and of course the letters of the alphabet.

Jacky's entry into the world of print was uneven. As a writer, Jacky was satisfying to both of us. He wrote short but complete stories of the "I love my cat" variety. He loved to sing, he loved to fight, and his self-confidence quotient was not high. He was having a hard time with reading. There were several books that he loved, which I had read aloud to the class or the class had all read aloud together from an enlarged-print version. These he could "read," or more properly "tell," and he loved to. He loved silent reading time, because he could flop down with these and feel successful. But as far as making sense for himself of new print, he could not. He wasn't a sight word learner, and he was having trouble with connecting letters and sounds, either in isolation or in context. This is where we were at the Christmas break, and his mother was not pleased. I will give her credit; she bought one or two books for him with every book order I sent home, but then she didn't read them to him! I have no idea if Daddy read them during his intermittent stays.

Jacky needed more time and he wasn't going to get it. There was no chance that Jacky would get to stay in first grade any longer than the normal one year, so I promised myself that after Christmas I was going to concentrate on him. I got out all the most exciting easy books available, of which the best (to my mind) were Brian Wildsmith's *The Cat on the Mat*, Theo LeSeig's *Ten Apples up on Top*, Eric Carle's *The Very Hungry Caterpillar*, Dr. Seuss's *The Foot Book*, and P. D. Eastman's *Are You My Mother?* (Now this list would also include *Mrs. Wishy-Washy* and *Cookie's Week*. Every day he and I read one of these and I tried to help him see, and hear, that if he knew the first sound in many words he could figure out what was happening. In *The Cat on the Mat*, for example, there is a wonderful illustration of each animal that comes to sit with the cat, and Jacky could glibly "read" this whole book just fine by looking at the illustrations. Then one day I covered up the pictures and he got very confused. He remembered that the dog came after the cat, but then said that *cow* was *goat*. This response was not helpful.

"Let's go back to the cat," I said. He flipped the pages back to the beginning. "Read those words first," I said, sweeping my hand under the sentence, "The cat sat on the mat."

> ## And suddenly there came the magic. All by itself, as it seemed to me, Jacky's right hand rose up and *finger-spelled* as he spoke the letters *c, a, t.*

"I can do this one," Jacky said confidently. He pointed to each word and read the sentence clearly.

"Great, Jacky," I said. "Now where's *cat* on this page?" He put his finger under the word. "Spell that word, just like it is there," I said, trying for some magic reinforcement, I didn't know exactly what.

And suddenly there came the magic. All by itself, as it seemed to me, Jacky's right hand rose up and *fingerspelled* as he spoke the letters *c, a, t.* Then, while I still held my breath, he said and signed the letters again, and sounded them, too! Fingers, voice, and eyes were all going at once. He nonchalantly started to turn the page and stopped. "Cover up the next picture," he commanded me, his stature and confidence enlarging with every breath.

Wordlessly, I did so, and he read the next page, fingerspelling and sounding the letters *d, o, g* appropriately, and on through the end of the book.

"Well," he said, flexing his hand, "I sure can read that one good."

"You sure can," I agreed, finding voice at last as the magic settled onto Jacky as normal.

"Can I read another one?" he asked. "I'll go find one for myself," he added, leaving me with a whirl.

Now, in the post-Jacky years, I know to suggest or even quietly model this method of connecting sign to sound. I have no idea why it happened, why it happens to other Jackys, what is actually going on as he and they connect the sight, movement, and sound elements of themselves to translate the printed word into their brains. I call it magic, because I don't know.

To me, all reading is magic; this triple-senses way is just a little more so. Lynessa Cronn, a colleague who teaches hearing-impaired children, tells me that this magic is often true for them as well: "Eric looks at his hand fingerspelling as he writes words; it's as if his hand is a separate entity he has no control over."

To me, all reading is magic; this triple-senses way is just a little more so.

Young children mimic. Everything they've ever done they've done by mimicry, and so when you begin to sign to a whole classful of hearing children, it is unlike signing to teachers or other humans. Children learn to talk and move and walk and eat, and everything else they do, with their bodies first. Many adults have sort of blotted out their kinesthetic talent over the course of their training as people. Many adults don't do much with their bodies at all, and even the joggers of our time do not move spontaneously, as children do, or in exploratory ways.

Grownups have learned the hard way that they aren't any good at the kinesthetic body-moving elements of this life. Most adults have some depressing story to tell about how their third-grade teacher convinced them they couldn't draw, for example. Alexander, of the terrible horrible day, had a teacher who didn't even like his *invisible* castle.

The same thing happens, maybe more often, with music. I meet many teachers who refuse to sing because somewhere along the line they were told that their voices weren't perfect. A lot of us were brought through school by elders who had a very high standard of art and music that most of us never came close to meeting. I could always carry a tune, so I wasn't blotted out as a musician; I certainly have a strong sense, however, that I am an utterly inadequate artist, and as for dance . . . forget it!

But children only know they are inadequate if we tell them they are. Most children who sing along with Raffi nowhere near the appropriate pitch think they are doing just fine, and indeed they are. Most children who lovingly create a whole painting out of red smears of random shapes have a better self-concept than Van Gogh or Michelangelo ever thought of having. They will only find out that they are off the mark if we let them know, and it is better to let them discover much later that their paintings and singings were, at the very worst, childlike.

In present educational jargon, the issue we are speaking of is "modalities." Modality differences, and our perceptions of them, are very real. Sign, like dance, is a manifestation of the kinesthetic modality, the one hearing American children use least in traditional language acquisition.

Sign is the reinforcement for young hearing children of the idea that what they have to say and, behind that, what is in their minds, can be brought out into a way of discussing, a way of doing, a way of communicating.

On a slightly deeper level, sign is the reinforcement for young hearing children of the idea that what they have to say and, behind that, what is in their minds, can be brought out into a way of discussing, a way of doing, a way of communicating. They've learned how to talk, they're learning how to write; they can also learn to sign. It is another reinforcement of the fact that language takes what's inside you out; that through language you can connect to other people and other things and other places.

What happened to Jacky was a combining of the three modalities of vision, hearing, and movement. Anne Green Gilbert, dance educator extraordinaire of Seattle, says that movement enhances learning, period. Children who dance can see themselves as kinesthetic, and can see themselves as successful with their bodies and not feel, as so many adults feel, afraid of that modality. In one sense, sign is dance. Watching someone sign a song, either silently or with voice, is like watching dance.

In that sense it can be just fun, although you have to be aware that it's a fine line; you don't want to be just having fun—or making fun—with someone else's language. To hearing-impaired persons, the luxury of three modalities cannot be taken for granted. Their language is acquired and used first with the other modalities, visually and kinesthetically. Instead of belonging in and growing out of the combination of speaking and hearing, it begins with sight and sign to which speech may or may not be added. Sight, in this context, includes facial and body expressions that hearing people are not nearly as good at. Facial expressions that extend or focus the meaning convey important nuances of understanding.

No one who does not have a disability can understand what it is like to have one. In addition, people who do not have disabilities—hearing-impaired, autistic, or whatever—look askance sometimes upon those who do. In particular, those who can hear have sometimes assumed of those who can't hear that they are not intelligent, either. Helen Keller's early years are the most well-documented example of this phenomenon that I can think of. When she learned to sign, her world learned that she had a mind even though she had no voice.

Children whose first language is sign, however, may have some of the same kinds of difficulties learning to write in English as children whose first language is Russian, or Cantonese, or Hmong. The difference in orthography matters only to children from other cultures who are literate in those other languages, but the relationship of that orthography to the phonetic structure of English is illogical to all young children who begin in another language. I recently had a conversation about this second-language with teachers at the Governor Baxter School for the Deaf in Portland, Maine.

"What am I supposed to write for a child who gives me his sentence in nonstandard language?" asked Lisa, one of the teachers who is Doing Words with the seven-year-olds at that school. "If Steven wants to have, 'The dog bit me' for his sentence, he will sign *me, dog,* and *bit,*" she explained, signing as she said those words. "If I ask him to say his sentence, that's what he'll sign. If I then write it on his sentence card, 'The dog bit me,' and sign back to him *the, dog, bit,* and *me,* he is very likely to tell me that he didn't say *the* in his sentence. What am I supposed to do? Sometimes I feel like it's too confusing for him, and I should write on the card, 'Me dog bit,' which is what he said."

I was nodding all through this story. "This is a hard problem," I agreed. "It's worried me for a long time about all children, hearing or not, and their incorrect and dialectical speech. I've finally settled on the belief that the written language has to be correct. The model of what they are seeing and using in writing has to be standard English. The real killer is that not only do hearing-impaired and immigrant children have to learn to speak a whole new language, be it ASL or signed English or spoken English, they also have to learn a written language that may be very different. It's not fair, but there it is."

"He'll tell me that what I wrote isn't what he said," Lisa repeated.

> **In English you speak or sign one way, but you write another.**

I nodded again. "He will, I agree. And you tell him that he's a good reader for figuring that out, first of all, and then this: In English you speak or sign one way, but you write another. Written English is another language."

"That's hard," said Lisa, and murmurs of concurring opinion slurred around the room.

"Yes," I said. "As if being deaf or ESL weren't hard enough. But how helpful are we being if we don't give them the language they have to write and read for the rest of their lives?"

It is not possible to be like a person with a disability. The separation can at least be eased, however, if members of the hearing community enter even partially into communication with those who do not hear. For this very social reason, sign is a neat thing to do with young children. The work of Linda

Bove on Sesame Street has opened this world to many children, and their schools can continue it. It can't hurt the hearing children at all (and may help society at large) to give them a glimpse into the language lives of others. It won't hurt us as a people to come as close as we can to accepting each other.

Both Jacky and Buddy are within the normal intelligence range, although because their proficiency on standardized tests is limited by their family backgrounds, that normalcy has not always been accepted. Both of them have spent some of their school time since grade one in tutoring situations of various kinds, but both of them will make it. Tara is another story, another kind of story.

The designations and initials for school children under the special education umbrella change fairly often; my own labels for the children who have problems, the Buddys and the Jackys, are rather simpler. For me such a child either will manage within the system, or will not. Tara was one of the latter sort.

Tara was already seven when she came to my class in October. Ours was the fourth school she and her little sister had been in already, in as many towns. After our school secretary had registered them, she brought Tara to my room and whispered, "No telling where her records are—she's moved around some."

Tara moved right around the secretary, and into the middle of the room, where she stood still, planted her feet, put her hands on her hips, threw back her head and said—or rather howled—"HOWWOOO! HEY KIDS! HELLOOO!"

Startled, the children turned from their various tasks and stared at Tara. She beamed, waved, smiled an enormous and toothless smile.

"Hey, kids," she went on in the friendliest way, at a slightly lower level of sound. "Whatcha doin'?"

The secretary raised expressive eyebrows, whispered "Good luck!" to me, and slipped back into the hallway. I stayed by the door and watched this amazing entry. Tara strode over to the alcove where Tiffany and MaryAnn were lying on the floor, half on a big piece of chart paper, surrounded by markers of various sizes and colors.

"Hey, you girl," Tara not-quite-shouted at them, hands still on hips, chin thrust out. "Whatcha doin'?"

"We're writing a story," replied Tiffany in her usual soft voice. Tara looked at her and the paper, her head twitching from the girl to the paper. Then she reached out a hand and pushed MaryAnn on the shoulder.

"Hey you girl," she repeated to MaryAnn. "Whatcha doin'?"

MaryAnn backed away from the pushing arm and looked over at me before she, too, answered. "Tiffany just told you," she said with only a slight impatience. "We're writing a story together."

"Gimmee marker, then," demanded Tara. "I c'n write a story together." And she grabbed the delectable pink marker from MaryAnn, jumped down to a squat on the paper, which ripped, and made wide sweeping marks on top of the careful printing already there.

The room erupted with shouts and statements of protest. I reached Tara before Tony, our resident self-appointed policeman, did, and turned her around, marker and all.

After several days, perhaps weeks, Tara accepted the fact that she could only "write" on her own "stories," but she had no understanding at all of what "writing" a "story" was. Her favorite thing to do was to listen to me read, and the rest of the time the days were a toss-up. When we got into sign, though, she learned the letters, she really learned which was which—in fingerspelling.

> **Sign, for hearing children, is a new way to talk, a new way to communicate in addition to talking, writing, and listening.**

She spent many minutes each day, then, looking at the name cards of things around the room—window, door, calendar, children's names on their desks, exit, and so forth—and said the letters as she fingerspelled them. Most of the time she was right.

She was with us for about six months, and then moved away again. Believe it or not, we missed her. Whatever else she may have picked up in the way of behavior or learning, at least she took the manual alphabet with her. I like to think it helped.

Notes: Connecting with Sign

Sign, for hearing children, is a new way to talk, a new way to communicate in addition to talking, writing, and listening. Sign uses instead seeing and moving, connecting the body to the brain. To combine the use of sign with the ordinary ways language is acquired and used is to increase the number of modalities children use so they enlarge their use of language, understand sound/letter correspondence, and read. The easiest way to begin is to teach:

- signs for yes, no, ready, my-name-is, fine, colors, please, thank you, may I go to the bathroom, wonderful, nice job

- the manual alphabet

- songs, such as color songs, and familiar songs such as *It's a Small World*
- repetitive number and alphabet songs such as *One Elephant Came Out to Play, Chicken Soup with Rice, Mary Wore Her Red Dress, The Wheels on the Bus, A Alligators All Around, May There Always Be Sunshine*

Use sign also as classroom management for

- giving directions
- transitions
- getting into lines
- making groups

Sign language corresponds to oral language, so it allows for much variation; all children, hearing and not, need to learn standard English as their written language. In English you may speak or sign in many "dialects" but you write in another, standard form.

6

Who Is Special?

I once saw—once—a wonderful, two-month-long study of medieval times done by the Chapter I students in a smallish elementary school. The children loved it, worked very hard, learned more than anyone thought even remotely possible, and used every imaginable angle, from leatherwork to cooking to shieldmaking to writing their own Knight stories, in this wide and deep study. On several occasions these children were cast as experts on the subject in their regular rooms and performed brilliantly.

Only the once. Before and after these two months there was and continues to be a lot of drill on short vowel sounds.

Chapter I students are named after a federal law which provides monies and teachers for children who are "behind." It is designed to catch up the children who aren't quite up with the others but who, in the estimation of the school, can be. This odd arrangement makes these children "special" but always working toward being not special, toward being regular and ordinary again, to outgrow Chapter I status.

These children were cast as experts on the subject in their regular rooms and performed brilliantly.

When I first began teaching there was no room in Chapter I—which was then called Title I—for children younger than second grade, so children who needed some help right off the bat first had to endure two whole years of failure in kindergarten and first grade. Then they could be noticed and, perhaps, helped. The program is a wonderful idea, and there can always be more time spent with the children who need the most help, but there are disadvantages to being a federal program. Chapter I spaces are often very creative. Chapter I teachers, because they are paid differently, often have an uncertain place on the staff. Chapter I students have to be tested often and often, to make sure that nobody is using federal money unwisely.

A Chapter I teacher I knew was very upset one year when the California Achievement Test scores came back for the building; there were only two children whose magic number fell below 33. Anyone below 33 was eligible for her help. Because she had no job if the children did well, she could not rejoice in their success—which was also, of course, hers.

Of all the people in our schools who need us to be sure to help them travel their own path, the neediest are the ones we designate as special. This euphemism is an odd kind, because although the needy ones are indeed special, we have always implied "remarkably able" or at least "remarkable" with that term. I used the word *special* as an incentive often when my children were younger: "We're going to have a special treat after we get all these weeds pulled." Popcorn, ice-cream, going to the fair—these are special. Mr. Rogers, too, who has been loving children on public television for many years, uses *special* in that rather old-fashioned, noneducationese way, when he sings about how special each of his young viewers is to him and to her- or himself, as well. He means unique, wonderful. He means that he thinks that each child is, in fact, a treat.

Children designated as *special* are not treats for the system nor, all too often, for themselves. The children enrolled in the special education programs, of which Chapter I is one, are the most rapidly growing population of all school subgroups, and most often they are the un-able, the most different, the ones we want to celebrate about the least. They have disabilities: academic, physical, mental, emotional, social. The older ones know they do not fit in; the younger ones suspect it. They know they are not so much special as they are different, not normal, inferior.

Most of their teachers, however, do think they are special. Most special education teachers are quite remarkably devoted to their children and believe in them quite fiercely. "What will become of them?" one teacher said to me. "They're chronologically ready for the junior high, but Oh, who will care about them there the way we do here?"

Sometimes, of course, the teachers lose sight of the children's needs.

In a certain class of thirteen children there are two teachers on a very tight schedule of moving children from workbook to workbook. The children work in groups of two or three going through a list of vocabulary words involved in a story written to emphasize homonyms. This is basal writing at its worst, because the meaning is squeezed through the filter of the linguistic peephole the authors of the book want, for no good reason, to emphasize.

Anyway, here are these children, ages 6 to 10, sitting with their teacher, concentrating on this book. One of them is actually able to read the words, that is, she can translate the letters into continuous sound that reflects the symbols on the page; she doesn't know what is happening to and with the characters in the story, however, and she, even she, has no idea what the double-entendres are all about. It takes me several minutes to get the meager point of this story myself.

These children are not connected to their reading, even the single child who can turn the letters into sounds. I have a strong sense that all of them think that this is what reading is. The children have picked up that reading a book is in a group; the teachers believe in groups, in making sure the children sit, quietly, in groups.

Of all places in schools, these classrooms where the children are designated as "special" are where the need is greatest for individual and child-centered work to be done. Doing Words and Big Books and a whole language adventure, as much as attention span and physical coordination will allow, will make a difference. Of course the organization will be different, of course as much movement and choice of activity as is possible in a whole language classroom for "regular" children may be less available to "special" children, but why should they be stuck with the old basals and the old dittos, or even new ones? That fill-in-the-blank stuff will never be part of their everyday lives. Connecting to their personal images and interests is just as important, certainly not less, for them as for anyone. Even if their memory span is not great enough to remember many Words at a time, the discussion about each day's Word with each child is bound to add to each one's self-esteem.

> **Classrooms where the children are designated as "special" are where the need is greatest for individual and child-centered work to be done.**

In Tina's developmental kindergarten the population is mixed. There is a friendly, if aggressive, nonverbal child; there is a child with severe cerebral palsy who cannot speak and who moves very little in her wheelchair; another girl plays mostly with dolls and the telephone, spanking the ones and verbally abusing her imaginary listeners; one boy has many problems with speech articulation, although he keeps trying to be understood; three others are within, barely, the "normal" range of behavior and ability for five-year-olds.

And this is a happy place. The children are invited to sit together and talk over their important events, and although Jason and Melody don't share their events, Jason, at least, is fascinated. They listen to a story or a poem that is not long or boring, such as "Jack Be Nimble, Jack Be Quick," and are

> **The children are invited to sit together and talk over their important events.**

invited to clap with it, repeat it, shout and whisper it, and act it out. Another day the poem is "Little Miss Muffet" and they act it out, too, taking turns eating the curds and whey, taking turns being the spider. They have a time to make spiders out of paper, or candles out of clay, and a time to work with blocks and dolls and paint. They learn to recognize their names, and to find their places in a circle for reading or at a table for working or in a line for snacks. They are busy, kept busy to be sure, but there is not a workbook in the place, nor any "coloring book" pages to fill in. Their lives are appreciated and as often as possible celebrated; next year, when most of them will go to an ordinary, "regular" kindergarten, we will hope that such celebration continues.

In another place, seven small boys come to the little room off the library to work with their Chapter I tutor, a tall, quiet young man named Clarence. He greets them and they him, sitting around a kidney-shaped table that nearly fills their space. Their Words folders are on the table and the boys take them up to read to each other—one reads to Clarence. Before they start Clarence takes Jason's writing book and holds it up.

"I want you all to see how neatly Jason was working on his sentence yesterday," he says. Jason smiles. "See how carefully he did it?" Jason beams. "Nice work, Jason." Jason struts a few paces away and back to the table. Clarence hands him his book, and Josh comes right up to Jason.

"Let's read by the door, Jason," Josh urges. They're off.

Clarence, meanwhile, is listening to Kyle read his Words.

Then two go to the computer behind the room divider and two go to the book and puzzle tables on this side of the divider. Dinosaur puzzles require concentration and conversation. Brad is deep into it, but Freddy, after talking with him for a minute or two, begins to wander. There is a table of big and small books next to the door, and Freddy chooses one, opens it, tosses it on the floor. Two more follow it; then he sees the big book version of *Dan the Flying Man* and says the title out loud. This is a book Clarence has read to the boys a few days before, and Freddy knows the story. He "reads" the book, turning each page and saying what is happening in the picture. Sometimes he "reads" in that odd voice children adopt when they are beginning to read, with the words all spaced apart and monotone; then he races in normal voice over another page.

Clarence is only peripherally aware of this, but he will ask Freddy for his Word next, and invites him to the table. Kyle has read all his Words and has talked to Clarence about his new one, *Donatello* (a Ninja Turtle) and has traced it. He has gone to read it to his friends; Jason has talked about his sentence for today and is writing it across from Clarence at the table.

"Freddy, come get your sentence now," says Clarence. Freddy tosses *Dan* on the floor, too, and comes to the table. "What are you writing today, Fred?" asks Clarence.

This routine is repeated for the

> **Before the half-hour period is over, they have all had individual conversation with their teacher, directed reading of powerful writing (their own) with each other, five or ten minutes of related language play . . . some painless phonics . . . and they depart.**

next twenty minutes, and then the boys all come back together and read their Words and writings to each other. Before the half-hour period is over, they have all had individual conversation with their teacher, directed reading of powerful writing (their own) with each other, five or ten minutes of related language play (computer, reading books, puzzle talk), some painless phonics ("What's *Donatello* start with, Kyle?"), and they depart (Freddy last, after picking up the books) as they arrived, smiling.

The teachers who don't read aloud to their students told me that the children wouldn't stay put long enough to have a whole book read to them. I can appreciate that. I would start with a song or a rap or a rhyme, long before I would read aloud. Big Books, or even wall-sized books, thrown onto the wall by an opaque projector, could be the next step. The younger children, for whom the reading in their book made no sense, who were very anxious because they didn't "get" the authors' meanings, could find meaning in print instantly.

In another town, there are thirty-one five-year-olds in an ordinary square classroom with short chairs, the alphabet over the chalkboard, windows on one side looking out on a sidewalk and a busy street. Most of them are Cambodian immigrant children, for whom such things as windows, streets, and bathrooms are very new, with a healthy subgroup of maybe ten or eleven Hispanic children, for whom bathrooms are ordinary, but for whom English

> **"I went to a restaurant I'd never been to before and I had the best burrito I ever had in my life before. Oh, it was good! So I think that is my special word for today: *burrito*."**

is still as baffling as it is for the Cambodians. Their comfortable and welcoming teacher of Japanese heritage has many kindergarten classrooms full of newly American children both behind and ahead of her.

"Today," she told the children one Wednesday, "I want to tell you about a special thing I did last night. I went to a restaurant I'd never been to before and I had the best burrito I ever had in my life before. Oh, it was good! So I think that is my special Word for today: *burrito*." She patted her tummy. "It was good. I went to this restaurant with my two friends and we had a good time, eating and talking."

While she talked, the teacher was holding up a long card of stiff paper, with a marker in her other hand. "Watch me," she directed the children. "I'm going to write my special Word on this card, so I can read it and keep it because it is important to me." She printed the word *burrito* on the card in big letters. Then she held it up for them all to see and traced each letter with her finger as she named it. "*B, u, r, r, i, t, o. Burrito.*

"Now I'm going to ask each of you for your special Word for today. Will you be thinking about it?" Solemn nods all around. "It might be somewhere you have been, it might be someone you like a lot, it might be something you like to play with—be thinking now!"

The children moved to their various work areas and the teacher took her cards and marker to the table. The children came, one at a time, to talk about their important Word. Paco came first.

Oh, the thrill of this! Paco leveled his liquid brown gaze at his teacher and looked at the blank card in front of her. "Can I have my friend on this card?" he asked, his head tilted. "Of course," she said. "Who shall I write on this card for you?" Smiling widely, Paco said, "My friend is Vutha." She wrote it; Paco burst out into a laugh with the joy of seeing the name of his friend Vutha. He did what the teacher asked, pretended his finger was a pencil and traced the letters on the card, bubbling with his laughter. His face was lit up with the joy of knowing that these squiggly lines, these letters on this card, were the name of his friend, and he could carry it off and read it to anyone and it would always be Vutha.

Of course you can never imagine which child Paco ran to right away, to show this Word and read it to. Then Paco brought Vutha back to the teacher, a Vutha eager to do this, too, and Paco told him he could get a Word, too, and Vutha did. And then the two of them laughed together, said their Words to each other, and began, in that joy, to learn to read.

I am sure that these children will enter English print and reading and writing more quickly and effectively by Doing Words than by many other methods now in use. In the classroom of Paco and Vutha, there were only three or four native languages; in other classes there can be many more.

My friend Mrs. I., for example, has a class of (often) twenty-nine kinder-gartners and within that number there are as many as eleven native languages. She used to struggle with this diversity, as she worked her way through all the letters and sounds, using one program after another designed to "motivate" children to be fascinated by phonics and sound-symbol correspondence. There were Alpha people for a few years, there were letter books, one a day, workbooks workbooks workbooks, and even little floppy senseless books of insipid stories, known as basal readers. The children who couldn't do English could get even less interested in the unconnected books and workbooks. Mrs. I. learned a few words of Farsi, a few of Mandarin, a few of Thai, and a lot of Spanish, but she knew that wasn't the answer. Individualized language instruction within the framework of the classroom society was what she needed. Then she found Doing Words.

> **"This is a scarf, Edizen," said Mrs. I. "I can give you *scarf* for your Word today, shall I?"**

Even on the first day the ESL children came to school, whatever that day was, Mrs. I. watched their play with other children and with the things around the room. After all the children who were speaking in English got their Words, she went over to Edizen. She greeted the Iranian five-year-old in Farsi. Edizen's apprehensive eyes lit for a moment. Her hands were stroking one of the dress-up table scarves, which had a synthetically silky feel to it.

"This is a scarf, Edizen," said Mrs. I. "I can give you *scarf* for your Word today, shall I?" She looked around the play area and saw Nicole, whose Word that day was *doll.* Nicole was at that moment holding the doll and hadn't yet taken her Word to the basket. Mrs. I. called her over, word card, doll, and all.

"What's this, Nicole?" she asked pointing to the doll. "Can you tell Edizen what this is?"

"It's a doll," said Nicole helpfully. "And here's *doll* too, look!" and she held up her card. "This says *doll.*" She ran her hand under the letters, just as she'd seen Mrs. I. do.

"Good job, Nicole," said the teacher. "Thanks." She turned to Edizen, her hands still on the scarf. "This is a scarf. Can you say *scarf*?"

Edizen held on to the scarf.

> ## "Read it to Nicole, now. Nicole, please read yours so she'll know what to do."

"And this is the Word *scarf*," Mrs. I. went on, writing it on a card with her marker. "Say *scarf*, Edizen." She touched the scarf and the card in turn and repeated the Word. Then Edizen repeated the Word, too.

"Great," said Mrs. I. "Read it to Nicole, now. Nicole, please read yours so she'll know what to do."

Nicole obliged, Edizen read, they both took their cards to the basket, and Mrs. I. turned to Adom, the Israeli boy who had been with them two weeks already. She found him in the block corner, playing towers-in-patterns with Luis, a completely bilingual Hispanic American.

"Did you get your Word today yet, Luis?" she began, continuing instantly with "Oh, yes I remember now. Good morning, Adom," she went on. "What's that you're making there?"

"Is tower," replied Adom clearly. He pointed to the cards she was holding. "Is Word today? *Tower*?"

"Certainly," replied Mrs. I., opening her marker. "Watch me write it."

And he repeated *tower* to two classmates before putting it in the basket. Later it would join *Luis, blocks, airplane, Jeremy, Itzhak, school,* and *friend* in his packet of Words that he reread every morning.

Mrs. I. has found that Doing Words gets ESL children involved with their new language quickly and connects them to things and people in their new environment, things and people important to them as they live their new lives. Each one's interests and personhood are taken very seriously, and they do exactly what the other children are doing.

What can be more special than that?

Notes: Special Cases

Most special needs children, including those in Chapter I, who are learning disabled rather than physically disabled need

- structure
- time organized in fairly small segments
- whole language and number studies
- predictability and repetition for comfort
- times when it is safe to laugh, show feelings, take risks

They profit and stretch best in a classroom where there is

- constant oral language use, lots of talk
- tactile and kinesthetic activity equal to verbal and print activity
- labeled print environment that is referred to often
- daily reading aloud, preferably patterned and well-written books
- song as a daily extension of language
- drama and movement in regular small, controlled doses
- hands-on extensions and reflections of language learning (paint, constructions)
- Doing Words, connecting the use of language to the children's lives, giving them ownership of the language about which they are learning
- skills (phonics, usage, punctuation) pulled from their own language and from the experiences of the class
- responsibility for successful transitions several times a day
- daily journal time for reflection or venting
- literature for reading, for maximumengagement

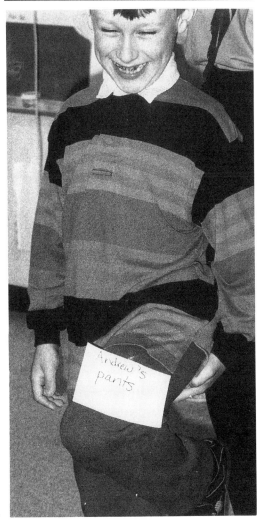

Some books about special children, to read aloud include

What Do You Do When Your Wheelchair Gets a Flat Tire?
   by Douglas Biklen and Michele Sokoloff

Nick Joins In by Joe Lasker

I Have a Sister, My Sister Is Deaf by Jeanne Peterson

Through Grandpa's Eyes by Patricia MacLachlan

Everybody Needs a Rock by Byrd Baylor

7

Poems Are Always Possible

One of the nicest things about any song is that it is also a poem, and most poems can be turned into songs if you feel like it. Poems without music are enormous fun, too, in as many forms as possible for as many reasons.

Working with people older than 25 or so can be a challenge because they believe that poetry is something very specialized and they know they can't do it. Somewhere along the line they have met a teacher or even a poet who convinced them of their inadequacy through complex analysis of a text or by the obscurity of some "poetic" language. (Although poets certainly don't have the patent on obscure language, we are more likely to assume that a poet's complex or abstruse language has some inner meaning, when in fact the words may be as poorly chosen as those in an interdepartmental memo.) Children, generally, have proportionally less of this lack of confidence, from some fear at high school age down to zero fear and full confidence at age six.

One way to begin a study of poetry is with song.

And one way to begin a study of poetry is with song. Children, even the bigger kids, always know and like a song if it's a popular one (especially a Disney one), and almost all of the songs little children sing they know by heart, sing very fast, and feel very competent about.

So I choose a song and sing it and then put the words on a paper (or chart or overhead) and ask what this text is. Someone will say it's a poem. Often the characteristics of this poem include rhymes at the end of the lines, or alternate lines, and often the beginnings of the lines will have capital letters. We talk a little about these characteristics.

There are nearly as many forms for poetry as there are poets, however, and an exhaustive list would probably fill this page. Many of them are much more difficult than a simple rhyming poem, but simple rhymes are very difficult for me, so I respect even the smallest verse that rhymes. How Pope and Milton and Ogden Nash do it at length I have no idea. So the next time I point out what a poem can be I use a song that doesn't rhyme, such as *This Land Is Your Land,* which has a clear rhythm and a clear message. We talk a little about these elements. It's always important to ask, "What do you hear?"

Becoming acquainted with various kinds of poetry is the first step. Being read aloud to is the best way to further this acquaintance, and indeed this may be another reason why some people feel so intimidated by the medium: nobody ever reads it aloud to them. It is nearly impossible to "get" the rhythm of something just from reading it silently, and my personal need is to hear a piece of poetry—or any writing—at least twice before I can feel that I've "heard" it through.

Then we begin to write. I strongly recommend Judith Steinbergh's *Beyond Words: Writing Poetry with Children,* and there are others, too, more every year, I'm sure. I've recently been directed to David Greenberg's *Teaching Poetry to Children,* but I haven't found it yet.

I like to begin with monsters. Read a book about a monster or a scary construct, so that the children in the group all have a similar idea, a similar set of words or description or pictures to draw from and build on, and then simply rework that now-familiar material into a more linear, "poetry" form.

Two good books to do this exercise with: Mercer Mayer's *There's a Nightmare in My Closet* and Robert Munsch's *A Promise Is a Promise.* Both books deal with a bogeyman kind of monster that children and other humans of any age can relate to. (The Munsch book has the added advantage of an Eskimo setting, so you can dive into some questions of culture comparing, too.)

In *A Promise Is a Promise,* a little Eskimo girl named Allashua doesn't believe in the Quallupalluit, monsters who live under the sea ice near her house. Everyone else, including Allashua's parents and younger siblings, fear these Quallupalluit because they like to take children away forever, under the sea ice; they are respected because they have always promised never to take any children who are with their parents. Because she doesn't think they are real, Allashua disobeys her parents and goes to the edge of the sea and taunts the monsters. They of course grab her and to save herself she promises to bring her brothers and sisters to them instead. Allashua is not a terribly sympathetic child.

> **The next time I point out what a poem can be I use a song that doesn't rhyme, such as *This Land Is Your Land,* which has a clear rhythm and a clear message.**

She returns home and confesses to her parents, who tell her she was not smart to tempt the Quallupalluit and then promise them her family, and then the mother makes a plan so that Allashua can keep her promise to the Quallupalluit and the parents can keep the children. Everything works out, I'm glad to say, so that the monsters never again come through the cracks in the sea ice.

After I read this story to them, I ask what they thought of it. Usually they want to tell me about Allashua, and about the monsters.

"Boy, my mom woulda spanked her so bad," one girl said.

"Yeah, she sure was naughty," said the next one.

"Naughty," I repeated, writing it on the board. "You think your mother wouldn't have liked what she did," I restated.

> **"Naughty," I repeated, writing it on the board. "You think your mother wouldn't have liked what she did," I restated.**

"No!" said the first one. "She did exactly what they had told her not to!" She squirmed a little. "I always get in *bad* trouble when I do that!"

"She did what they told her not to," I wrote.

"And she was wrong about the Kalla—Quill—whatever," added another one. "They were really real."

"Wrong about the Quallupalluit," I wrote, and "really real." I turned back to the group. "What did you think of them?" I asked.

Many voices answering at once: "Ugg-LEE!"

The pictures in *A Promise Is a Promise*, of course, show the features of the Quallupalluit in gruesome detail, but I find that generally the children don't notice the pictures as much as the words in the story. The nonvisual details are very clear:

"Do we know anything about what these creatures smell like?"

"They smell rotten, the book says," replies Maria.

"Like dead whales in the summertime," corrects Sally.

"Yeah, like I said," repeats Maria, "rotten."

"And what the Quallupalluit sound like?"

"I think they talk soft, but kind of mean."

"Robert Munsch says they sound like snow blowing over the ice."

"You know she shoulda known they were there when she heard that sound, 'cause there wasn't any wind."

> **After a wait I make my face mysterious, go back to the chart, and carefully and obviously trace capital letters over the first letter of the first word in each line.**

I list all these attributes of smell and sound, and various descriptors for their appearance—"green fingers," "long straggly hair like seaweed, waving,"—on the chart until it's full or until we run out of ideas, and then we read, chorally, the whole list.

"Well, now, what shall we do with this?" I ask them. "There's not much point in writing a story about these creatures, because Robert Munsch already did that. So here's all this stuff about the monsters in a list. . . . "

At this point it will depend on how much poetry you have read and shown to the children. Perhaps someone will say, tentatively, "It could be a poem because there aren't any sentences," and perhaps no one will say anything. After a wait I make my face mysterious, go back to the chart, and carefully and obviously trace capital letters over the first letter of the first word in each line. I look at the group eagerly.

"Now can we read it again?" I asked them. This is what we read:

Quallupalluit

Really real
Ugly
Smell rotten
Like dead whales in the summer time
Talk soft, but kinda mean
Like snow blowing over ice
Green fingers
Waving like seaweed
Like to catch children
Scary

"There! Nice job of reading," I tell them, as I always do. "We wrote a poem about Robert Munsch's monsters. Pretty neat, don't you think?" Various offhand agreements—these are second-graders, after all, with none of the grown-up inhibitions about poetry that I share—rebound around the class.

The next thing that will happen in this room is a discussion of monsters, personal monsters that the children have in their minds. If I ask carefully and steer them into their unique ways of looking at their world, then I don't get too many Ninja Turtle clones. Seven- and eight-year-olds can get pretty eloquent about monsters, and after a little discussion I ask them to draw—color, chalk, whatever they like—pictures of the monsters they have in their heads. (There's no reason, except the constraints of time, why these monsters can't be made in three dimensions.) This part can take a while, and then they can show them off to each other.

After reviewing the poem we did together, we'd identify the senses—sight, smell, hearing, touch—and talk about names for the monsters; then each writer would set out in a list the way his or her monster looks, sounds, feels, with one word at the end like our *scary* to sum up.

On another day, perhaps the next day, we would set about the task of writing individual poems about the monsters the children have made. After reviewing the poem we did together, we'd identify the senses—sight, smell, hearing, touch—and talk about names for the monsters; then each writer would set out in a list the way his or her monster looks, sounds, feels, with one word at the end like our *scary* to sum up.

Here is Adam's:

Kingaloouck

Hairy orange hands
Purple eyeballs stick out
Looks like a gorilla
Smells like mold in the refrigerator
Smelly feet like the creek
Likes to eat hamsters and rats' blood
Mean

and Rachel's:

The Blue Water Monster

It is covered with light-blue curtains
Green shiny eyes
Hungry all the time
Smells like the swimming pool
It makes my nose itch
Creeps after girls on the beach
Sneaky monster

Rachel, as you see, was much more connected to the seascape of Munsch's creatures, and not too clear about leaving out the first parts of the sentences; Adam was into blood and King Kong, and seemed to have the clearer idea of pattern. As first poems, though, these were delightful to me, to them, to their principal, and to their parents. More poetry followed, and they began to collect their own and their own favorites copied from books, from the teacher's charts, and from their friends. Build your own anthology; why not?

Metaphor is the heart of poetry. Metaphor, as I use the term, is any set of words used to describe something for which those words are usually not used. Hair and song, for example, are totally unrelated in the normal course of living. There are any number of ways to introduce this idea, and of course the best way to introduce young writers to metaphor is to read to them.

> **"And any set of words that is used to make the picture of something clearer, which has nothing to do with that something normally, that is called *metaphor*."**

In *Animals, Animals*, Eric Carle's wonderfully illustrated collection of poems, there are several poems that illustrate this idea. (I have used them with children ages 6 through 12.) Particularly wonderful is a D. H. Lawrence poem about a bat, in which he says that the bat's wings are "like a glove, a black glove thrown up at the light/And falling back." Another, by Kipling, says that a camel's neck "is a hairy trombone/Ra-ta-ta-ta! is a hairy trombone." It's easy for children to say, after you have read these a couple of times, what the thing is that the poet uses which has nothing to do with the subject, that is, bats or camels. "A glove!" they shout. Some of them love to stretch out their own necks and point toward them, to be sure I know that they know. "And any set of words that is used to make the picture of something clearer, which has nothing to do with that something normally, that is called *metaphor*," I tell them. "D. H. Lawrence helps us to see the bat more clearly by using the image of a black glove as a metaphor for the wings of the bat."

It sounds simple, and it is. Look for more of these, in poetry or prose (or send the students into their own reading to find some) and don't forget the obvious, such as Jane Yolen's snow in *Owl Moon*, "whiter than the milk in a cereal bowl." And then, turn the reading around into writing.

With younger children, I often begin with the bat and the camel, and invite them to make a poem with me about an animal of my choice (usually a turtle, because I like turtles, and I give that as my reason). "What's your favorite animal?" is a no-lose question in any elementary classroom, so the subject is there.

> **We make a web . . . about turtles on the board, with as many spokes as they are old—six for first graders, ten for fifth graders, and so on.**

We make a web (or a list, but I am personally addicted to webs these days) about turtles on the board, with as many spokes as they are old—six for first graders, ten for fifth graders, and so on. I ask them to help me fill up the ends of the spokes with facts and feelings about turtles, and soon there are many words there. "Leather eggs," "slow," "land and water," "eat fruit," "ancient," "green or brown," "carry own house."

Then I draw one more spoke and put a puffy cloud at the end of it for my metaphor. I step back and look at the web. "Now what image totally unrelated to turtles can I use for my metaphor?" I ask myself. I keep talking to myself, out loud, as I reread the web and choose the order of the poem. This simple trick is metacognitive work that can help children figure out how *they* think! And then there is the list, which is a poem because I capitalize the lines:

> Slow
> Silent,
> Ancient,
> The turtle leaves her eggs
> Leathery eggs
> In the sand
> And walks her house away
> A walking quilt.

I end the poem with a metaphor ("What metaphor did I use?" I ask them), and because of my example, some of the children saved theirs for the end, too. Some of the following poems, done by third-graders in September, were pretty boring until that kicker line at the end, which only means that the children were discovering another trick of writers, to surprise the reader into rereading.

Raccoon

I like the raccoon because
he is cute.
He has a long tail with
gray and black fur.
He washes his food
in the stream.
A gourmet in the wild.

(the Lion)

When I think of a Lion
I think of a king
a king with a yellow robe
and an orange crown
and the ferocious body
with teeth of gold
and a big heart for all
all for the lions
and all the lions look up to him
Like a hero.

I leave entirely aside the question of metaphor vs. simile. My goal here is not "The Learner Will Discriminate between Metaphor and Simile." My goal, which we reach often and often, is to hear "Look! Look! I wrote a poem! Wanna hear it?"

Another fairly surefire vehicle for poetry is color. There is a delicious little book called *Red Is Best,* by Kathy Stinson and Robin Baird Lewis, in which a little girl explains patiently to the reader the reasons why red is best—for pajamas, barrettes, boots, paint, and other important parts of her life—in metaphorical language. Her red boots, for example, take bigger steps; her red barrettes make her hair sing.

Kids get this idea. Actually the younger the children, the more easily they get it, since they live in metaphor and simile most of the time as they are working to connect the disparate pieces of their world. So I ask them to think about their favorite color, and while they are thinking I start a webbing on the nearest large surface. I almost always choose to do mine on the color brown, since very few children ever choose it as their favorite color.

Far from being too difficult for beginning writers, then, poetry is a naturally easy way for them to use language powerfully and succinctly, even when they are very young. Started then, it will last them a lifetime.

Notes: Poems

First, last, and always

- become acquainted with poems
- read poems aloud to your class, all ages, often, at least weekly, if not daily
- keep a class notebook of the poems
- remember that songs are always poems, and poems can be songs; sing

Next,

- write poems, as many kinds as you want with as many patterns as you like
- understand the power of poetry to shift our vision

Monster poems will hit the spot with primary children.

- Begin easily with reading a monster book.
- After reading, list the attributes of the monster.
- Capitalize the first word of each line and call it a poem.
- Read it chorally.
- Ask the children to draw their own monster.
- Ask them to write its attributes in a list.
- Share the drawings.

Read color poems, to connect feelings:

- Read *Red Is Best* or some of *Hailstones and Halibut Bones*.
- Web and write a group poem about a color.
- Ask the children to work in groups of three to four to web and write their own poems.
- Share the poems.

A list of books to tempt the student poets and the teacher:

A Promise Is a Promise by Robert Munsch

When We Were Very Young by A. A. Milne

There's a Nightmare in My Closet by Mercer Mayer

Red Is Best by Kathy Stinson

A Light in the Attic and other collections by Shel Silverstein

Rose, Where Did You Get That Red? and others by Kenneth Koch

Hailstones and Halibut Bones by Mary O'Neill

Animals, Animals collected by Eric Carle

8

The Outer Workings of the Writing Process

Prewriting, Drafting, Revising, Editing, Publishing

When we were doing that turtle poem in chapter 7, I used what I call the web-to-text strategy. It is a way to prewrite, to plan a piece of writing before you actually start writing it. What I love best about it is that the number of spokes out from the central idea in the middle is always the number of the student's age. This approach has two enormous benefits: First, it is organic to the child, not an arbitrary requirement by the teacher, and the number of ideas is finite—at least to begin with. The second benefit of this ploy is that children often do have more ideas, and then it is they who say, "I'm going to add some more spokes to my web, okay?" or "Can I write more than these things?" These are welcome questions, don't you think?

"Where were you?" "Who else is in this piece?" "What does whatever-it-is look like?" "Will your reader know when this happened?"

If by chance a student is having trouble filling up the spokes (not nearly as common an occurrence as the reverse), the most generic nudges will be helpful. "Where were you?" "Who else is in this piece?" "What does whatever-it-is look like?" "Will your reader know when this happened?"

Web-to-text is useful for many writers, and practically foolproof with reluctant or frightened writers. I have taught it to many children and their teachers, although I am careful to tell the teachers that they can put as many spokes as their kids are old, not themselves. I like to think that webbing allays

> ## She will never believe she is a writer if she never has to think of her own topics.

fears more thoroughly in grownups, even if they have to do it several times before they can accept how simple and helpful it is.

This activity is, as I say, one of my favorite prewriting strategies. The other two are talking and thinking. Before prewriting can begin, though, there has to be a topic. Topic choice is the biggest problem in the shift from teaching writing as we were all taught to write, and teaching writing as a process the children own. If your students are ever heard to whine, "What do you want me to write about?" you will know that you haven't managed the shift yet.

It's much easier, in many ways, just to give 'em ideas. Have you ever heard yourself say, in response to that whine, "Weeell, you could write about . . . " or the slightly more direct, "Why don't you write about . . . ?" These don't sound so bad, you think, because after all you're not telling them what to do, you're only *suggesting*. But the student will hear it as your expectation; she may very well stop looking inside herself for another idea. After enough days and weeks and years of this "suggesting," you may find your students on what Donald Graves calls "writers' welfare." They will have insensibly come to expect an idea handout from you every day. This state of affairs is, for one thing, exhausting for the teacher; mostly, overwhelmingly, it is damaging to the student. She will never believe she is a writer if she never has to think of her own topics. My extrapolation of that last statement is that it will be harder for her to think she is anybody if she doesn't believe in herself as a writer.

Being an author begins with thinking what you are going to write about. Children who aren't used to finding their topics in their own heads and their own lives may need some help. They don't need topics; they just need help finding theirs.

I have a wonderful list of generic topics that I occasionally use with older children and often use with adults. They are called thinkabouts:

  a time you were sure you were right
  a time you went somewhere and didn't know anyone
  the best birthday you ever had
  a difficult decision you had to make
  a time when you were really scared . . . happy . . . embarrassed . . .

If every writer in the class keeps a list of possible topics somewhere in or on his writing folder, once a week or so the teacher can throw out one of these and ask the students to write their idea on their topic list. The first one might turn up on Joe's list as "Sunset Beach," by which he means the time the whole gang went to the beach and put their blankets too near the shore (against his advice) and the radio got soaked. It might turn up on Sandy's list as "Permanent," the time she wanted to have curly hair and her mother told her she wouldn't like it and she didn't. These generic suggestions trigger ideas that are totally personal and eliminate completely the whine, "I can't think of anything to write about." The teacher needs to keep her own list, too, of course, but it is of her own ideas for herself.

> **The teacher sets the basic rule, to be sure, that there will be lots of writing done in this room, but the *what* and the *when* and, most importantly, the *how* will be the province of the student.**

The teacher sets the basic rule, to be sure, that there will be lots of writing done in this room, but the *what* and the *when* and, most importantly, the *how* will be the province of the student. The teacher must provide paper, ambience, light, confidence, writing implements, approval, rules for having conferences with each other, encouragement, examples of writing in many different genres, quiet, instruction in the mechanics of English when necessary, the model of herself as a writer, the requirement that writing be done, and the opportunity to publish. The teacher does not provide constant correction or "what to write about." The teacher is not the sole audience for the writing.

Most primary children don't need this web-to-text stuff, this prewriting and brainstorming for ideas and a simple way to put their ideas down. Children who have been Doing Words since early kindergarten have been choosing what is important to them every single day, so when they get to writing continuous text they trust themselves to have ideas. Many of their writings are similar, many of them are very short, undeveloped stories or descriptions of their friends or their pets or their TV shows (some of those are *long* but equally undeveloped). Sometimes these repetitive stories are very boring for the teacher, sometimes the teacher wants the child to move faster along a wiggly path called "story development," but these are issues of drafting and revision, not of prewriting and topic choice. Even management is a snap after the philosophic shift to believing that the children have ideas and can use them to learn.

Managing the writing process work of thirty people, any age, is not as easy as choosing a workbook page or two every day. There are, however, any number of ways to keep the writing of children organized and in one place. Ordinary manila file folders are adequate for kids to keep their drafts in once they get going, and in second grade and up the children can use the front of the folder for a topic list. Gloria's folder has the numbers 1 through 17 straggling down the left side, and entries next to several of these numbers: "The Kittens," "My Birthday," "The Mermaid and the Human," "My Dog Silky," "Dolphins," and about ten others. She has put some large, deliberate checkmarks next to a few of these, which means she has already used those ideas for a draft.

> **Generally speaking, I think each child should have not only the privacy of keeping her own folder but also the responsibility of keeping it accessible and intact.**

Depending on the contents of the school's supply closet, I feel the most organized when I can begin with a pocket folder for everyone. Two pieces of 12 by 18 inch oaktag, stiff folder-weight paper, one wrapped around a long side of the other, can be stapled or taped so that there are four pockets. The two inner ones can hold drafts, the two outer ones can hold topic lists, editing checklists, spelling books, and whatever else a packrat writer might need. With a particularly packrat or destructive group I've used a hanging pendaflex-file system to advantage, so folders don't get shredded in desks; generally speaking, I think each child should have not only the privacy of keeping her own folder but also the responsibility of keeping it accessible and intact.

I have found, too, that a stamp pad and date-stamper are not only fun but can be very helpful to both children and teachers. The children get a chance to bring closure every day to their writing by stamping the paper unobtrusively where they left off. The teachers get to see clearly how the students are using the time, and what writing is done daily.

When writing time begins, the children get out their writing folders. For the first several minutes of writing time, each one is reading something of his own to someone else, in little pockets of two or three all over the place—under desks, on tables, at seats, leaning on window sills. I am doing comparatively boring things such as sending the lunch count to the office, finding my own writing folder and my pen, making sure there is glue available at the publishing shelf. The children go to their writing spots when they finish reading and I begin circulating to find out who's doing what. For my own peace of mind I carry a checklist on a clipboard. I use a very basic grid for this checklist, with names of children down one side and days across the top, usually in six or seven vertical columns so that the writing history it contains will roll over a week in one direction or another.

Weekends are proportionally less of a hiatus as children grow older, but they are still two days out of the pattern. At the beginning of writing time every day, first thing, I go to each student, ask what she or he is doing during writing today, and make a note. I write *N* for someone who is starting a new piece, as in "*N* Alison's birthday," or "*N* star wars V," and *ct* for someone who's going on with the same thing. In a class of thirty there are occasionally as many as two who say, "I don't know," so in the space by those names I make a big circle. "I'll be back when I've seen the others," I tell them, and continue on my way. Generally speaking, this circumnavigation of the landscape takes between five and eight minutes. I get a commitment from everyone about where they are and what they are up to, and then I go back to the circled names, if there are any, to give

> **"Billy, can you help me spell all these dinosaur names right?" "Karen, listen to this and tell me if it's powerful or not." "Courtney, do you think the pink marker on the front or the green is best?" "Jacob, help! I think I lost my story, it's not on the screen anywhere!"**

a brief nudge. Some squares will have the note *R* because the student is revising; some will say "*E*—Andrew," because the student is editing with Andrew; some few will say *P* for publishing.

"What are you working on today?" the same old question, asked of everyone from middle first graders to groups of teachers I work with. Writing, thinking, talking it over, looking things up—all this work then continues for all but fifteen minutes of the allotted time. During the working part of this writing workshop, some children may have peer conferences about any element of the process: "Billy, can you help me spell all these dinosaur names right?" "Karen, listen to this and tell me if it's powerful or not." "Courtney, do you think the pink marker on the front or the green is best?" "Jacob, help! I think I lost my story, it's not on the screen anywhere!" Students ask each other nearly everything, and most of them can find their answers from each other. They learn from each other what works in their writing, and from me how to respond usefully to each others' writing.

If the writing time is set for forty minutes, the first ten minutes of the time is full of little checks and little conversations between the teacher and each of the children, some of them almost mini-prewriting conferences. The next ten minutes are absolutely quiet, while everyone, including me as daily as I can, writes. These are the prewriting and drafting steps or levels or stages of the writing process, not looking wildly different from what children in schools have always done; the difference so far is in the students' ownership of the topics and the styles in which they are writing. This may take some growing time. You can't say to students, any students, but particularly those who have been tightly controlled all year by their teachers, "Well, you've read

a lot of well-written books; now you can write." You might as well say to your own ten-year-old offspring, "Well, you've ridden with me to the store nearly every day of your life; now drive there yourself." Writing time will happen every day, and it will be understood that everybody writes and that the teacher will want to know what is going on.

The next big discovery is that every piece of writing begun does not have to be published, and the related discovery is that the first draft of a piece, although it may be ended, is not necessarily finished. The first of these is usually more welcome to students than to teachers; the second represents the heart of the writing process, the *sine-qua-non* of the shift from assignments and products: revision. Revision is so important that it will have a chapter all its own, and we will skip blithely over it now into the quagmire of editing, with a short rest on the hummock of student publication journey-records. In the time frame of writers' workshop, a revision conference may happen with me, or several small-group peer revision conferences may happen for the third ten minutes or so. If the children run their own revision conferences, which they certainly can be taught to do in fifth grade, I can use the time to have individual conferences with individual writers. For the last ten minutes, people can share what they have in progress or we can have a minilesson about some aspect of the process, the language, or the writings themselves.

> **"Revision is what it says, and editing is what it looks like on the page,"** I say to children.

Perhaps once every two weeks I choose to do a bigger writing lesson, about some aspect of the process, about strategies for a particular genre, or about some particular snarl of the English language. On those days there is only the check-in and the drafting time; the lesson will take twenty minutes. One of the first such lessons I encourage teachers to teach is about editing. It is the content of many of these lessons that is most likely to reflect the stated curriculum objectives of the school district for reading, writing, spelling, English usage, grammar, and punctuation.

We are empowering children during these forty minutes to believe in themselves as writers, to choose their own topics, and to choose when and what to publish within the framework of our expectations of genre studies: What is their responsibility within or in response to that empowerment? In theory, as we give children the responsibility for choosing the shape of their writing lives, they will take pride in their work and choose to take responsibility for making sure that the public version of their writing (also known as "final copy," "publishing") is correct. This pride is the ideal. The reality is that children have often been so well trained by the systems they grow up in not to think for themselves that they can't take this responsibility. They generally say, squirming, that they "dowanna." The problem is that they don't know how.

Editing, in my understanding of writing process, isn't like the editing a publishing company does. That's more like revision, which is concerned with content. Editing for classroom purposes is rather like proofreading, what a professional copy editor does after all the changes and adjustments in meaning have been made. "Revision is what it says, and editing is what it looks like on the page," I say to children; one young colleague of mine has a version that's even simpler: "Revision is to hear, editing is to see." I like that, too.

Editing comes after revising and before publishing. If a piece is not going to be published, it doesn't need to be revised or edited. It does, however, need to be legible at all times. For that reason only, I usually try to glance over as much of the writing that has gone on as I can before the folders are put away. If the writing can be readily deciphered, so that both the student and I will be able to retrieve it the next day, fine. If it

> **She can put post-it notes on the papers as she reads them, one with a positive comment and one with a question.**

can't, the problem is probably either a lack of ending punctuation or spelling. I tell the writer to fix as many periods and misspelled words as he is old before he puts it away. It is my intent, nearly always accomplished, to read over the current writing of one-fifth of the class every day; if James's is illegible, then I must take a minute the next day to make it clear to James that he must first make this writing clear to *me* before he does anything else. Writing that doesn't communicate is not doing its job.

An intermediate-grade teacher can plan to take home with her six writing folders each night (making her class total thirty—some years she might have to take home seven); this system will keep her pretty current with everyone's writing. She can put post-it notes on the papers as she reads them, one with a positive comment and one with a question. The kids will know which night is their night, so to speak, and this system gives her a surmountable amount of work and also a weekly deadline for the writers in her class. These comments are all *for revision only*. Suspend the editing pencil until the student has chosen to publish.

As I've wrestled with this editing business for the past several years (during which time, in my mind, it has been woven with and then separated from the major issues of spelling), I have concluded that I have to remember two things about editing. First, it averages more teachable moments than any other single activity in my class. Second, it takes a loooong time.

It has traditionally been the task of the teacher to red-pencil, highlight, or simply fix all the errors of punctuation, capitalization, and grammar. (She has traditionally also fixed sentence order, powerful language, organization, voice, and meaning as well, but since those are elements of revision we will ignore them here.) Because punctuation, capitalization, and grammar become more complex as children grow as

Because punctuation, capitalization, and grammar become more complex as children grow as writers, the editing task becomes more complex, as well.

writers, the editing task becomes more complex, as well. More responsibility for editing falls to the writer, although the role of the teacher as editor is never over.

The primary writer of six and seven and eight who is publishing a piece of writing usually needs only to deal with ending punctuation and capital letters, with occasional forays into quotation marks and their accompanying paragraphing rules. Because the idea of a sentence is always in front of the young ones' eyes as they are Doing Words, the question "What goes at the end of this sentence?" has meaning for them. If they have learned, instead, to create text from a webbing sentence by sentence, they have also learned the concept of what a sentence is. I teach, in a full group with a big chart as a lesson, that every sentence has to have ending punctuation. I teach this first on the big chart of a story we have written together that I have neglected to punctuate. I have different children come to the chart and put the periods (or exclamation points or, rarely, questions marks) where they go. Then we go back to the beginning and put a capital letter on every word that follows a period. It's amazing how much better the writing looks.

But you can't say, "Well now, all the books you read or look at have been edited, you know, so now edit yours" any more than you could say, "Write now." Editing has to be taught. Do this chart (or overhead) lesson with all ages to begin to teach (or review) what editing is. It's fun. Use content appropriate to the age, cursive instead of print when it's the preferred medium, and teach editing.

Then, when she has decided to publish a piece, I can sit with each primary writer and ask her to "read it and stop at the end of a sentence." The writer takes a pencil and puts the periods in, every one. Then she goes back to her place and puts the capitals next.

That would be the first editing session, and probably won't begin to cover the whole piece if it's longer than about four sides of paper with printing on them. After this session of editing and the writer's work on the periods and capitals at her place, the piece goes back into the editing box.

I don't write on the child's paper at all, at all, except to note lightly what day it is when we do some editing on it. I reserve five or six minutes every day to edit with the child whose paper is on the bottom, make a note in its margin about what day it is, and put it back in the box. Notice that I always edit "with" the child. It takes a long time, perhaps a week, to edit a piece. The process goes on, though, because there is always something else that the writer is working on. Everything doesn't stop just because there is a piece in the editing box.

> **"I'm editing with Peter," or "Angel is editing with me after I finish this page." I dutifully note "E-Peter" and "E-Angel" on my list.**

When the writers have been at this for a year or two, they can sit with each other to do this punctuation and capitalization checking. You can provide them with a "Peer Editing Checklist" if you like and are not averse to using more paper (or you can laminate a form to be reused), which the writer and the editor both have to sign or initial, for yet another moment of taking responsibility.

By the time they are ten, the children who have been writers for four years can be responsible for using a checklist of editing items on their own first, then using a friend and a peer list, then bringing the piece to the teacher for what has (unfortunately) become known as "the teacher edit." It becomes commonplace to hear, when I go around with my check-in list first thing, "I'm editing with Peter," or "Angel is editing with me after I finish this page." I dutifully note "E-Peter" and "E-Angel" on my list.

When these older writers have done their best and had help from a friend, then the piece goes into my editing box with the peer checklist attached to it. The shape of this peer checklist depends on many factors, including what the teacher feels are the important elements of the English language for her grade level and has in fact taught to the students. (It is totally unfair to ask anybody to edit for a skill or a usage that they've never heard of!) Gloria's class, for example, had a list that included capitalization of the first word, names, and I; ending punctuation; commas in a series; paragraphs in conversation. It changed a couple of times in the course of the year, too.

Some of the teachers I have worked with, teachers of several elementary grades, use a publication checklist, a "journey to publication" sheet that accompanies a piece from prewriting to publication. Each of the teachers has tailored the journey sheet to her own style and to the individual classes each year. As a piece is drafted, discussed, revised, and edited in various ways depending on how a teacher and a class want to make themselves accountable, boxes on the journey sheet are checked off until the piece is in the editing box.

Notice that none of those editing lists has spelling on them. Spelling, as I said in chapter 2, is a separate problem.

Give the six-year-old a personal spelling book and insist that it be used, at least as many times as the child is old if that child has trouble with the idea. In a three-page story, finding six words is not too hard, nor is it too imposed. When the child is ten, she can find ten words she's not sure of during writing every day, but no more than ten. Whether you use these words as spelling words, too, that is, as part of a spelling program to escape from Zaner-Bloser and others is another question. The point of a personal spelling dictionary is, once again, in another dimension, to teach the child responsibility. In addition to teaching spelling, pattern, and responsibility, keeping a spelling book also teaches phonics, and will continue to do so even into third grade.

> **The point of a personal spelling dictionary is, once again, in another dimension, to teach the child responsibility.**

It will not be necessarily true that, because the child has the correct spelling in his word book, he will use it correctly all the time. The heat of the writing moment at any age transcends these details in the drafting stages, and I expect it to; in the cold light of editing, however, the spellings are there or can be put there easily for the child to correct in the editing stage.

Not that the child will necessarily, either, always spell the simplest words correctly. Have you ever listened and watched as a child learns to speak? Once she gets into whole sentences she pretty much mimics the sentence and verb structure of the people around her and it sounds pretty good. As she feels more confident in speaking, she will begin to grasp that there are certain rules for the way the language goes together—words that tell what happened yesterday usually have *ed* on the end of them, for example. So this child who, at age two and three, used correct English, now at age five is saying things like "we singed a song," and "I goed to the park." Parents tear their hair.

This phenomenon happens with spelling, also, for all ages. It happens, too, with content and "interestingness" of writing, especially as the child is learning new ways of writing, new genres in which to say what she wants to say to the world. The teacher of writing process may find this to be true after she starts the writing workshop into motion. Regression, perhaps, is what the teacher of writing process will think, and tear her hair. Children may start writing much simpler pieces than they had been doing, with much simpler language and plot than they had been using.

Wait it out. They are experimenting. They are learning. Keep telling them what they are doing right, and keep teaching them what they need when they need it. If you've done it well, they'll be such powerful and empowered writers that they will leave you behind, in the dust. Hooray.

Notes: The Outer Workings

The steps of the writing process are:

Prewriting

- Think.
- Talk to a friend about what is on your mind, what is special, what you've been doing, what you know about spiders.
- Web (with as many spokes as you are old) a topic you think you'd like to write about, remembering the 5 Ws (who, what, where, when, why).
- Keep a topic list in your writing folder.

Drafting

- Write; or choose an order for the information on the web; make a sentence of each piece to create a text.
- Use your personal dictionary.

Revision

Revision is the central task of writing as a process; see chapter 9.

Editing

- Teacher and one child edit for what the child knows.
- Begin by reading your piece aloud, putting in periods, then putting in capitals you need.
- After two years of writing process, edit with a peer before you edit with the teacher.
- Be responsible for checking the spelling of as many words as you are old.

Publishing

- Remember that not everything you write will be or needs to be published; the ratio of drafts to publications will probably be 10 to 1 in grades 1 through 3, slightly less in grades 4 through 6.

- Use a journey sheet or publication checklist for a piece you want to publish.

- Reading aloud to another class or to the principal is a form of publishing.

Management for the Teacher

- Use a check-in checklist at the beginning of every writing time, recording what stage of the process the piece is in, what it is about, and if a revision conference is needed.

- Plan with the students how many pieces and in what genres you will expect them to publish each year.

- Have a silent writing time of about ten minutes after you have done your check-in.

- Meet with three or four writers in a revision conference.

- Have five minutes of editing time with a writer or two.

- Share your writing.

- Every ten to twenty days, do a lesson after silent writing and before or instead of sharing, or alternate several days of lessons with several days of open writing practice.

9

Writing for Revision

A writer gets an idea, sometimes makes a few notes, on a web or not, about this idea, sometimes doesn't, or maybe talks about it a little with someone. Then comes the writing, just writing writing writing until the writer runs out of things to say about it. Then comes more talk, which is generally much more successful with another person, although it can be done alone. At this point the writing must be read aloud, too, preferably by the writer. The talk about the writing here is focused and designed to help the writer polish the piece, by changing some words, angles, sequence, ideas, conclusions, leads. This work is the heart of the whole writing process adventure: revision. It is the most difficult, the most frustrating, and the most wonderful thing I do now with both children and teachers. It is after this process that the concentration on where the periods go, and all the other picky proofreading and editing things—picky but necessary—such as spelling, must be done if the piece is to be published.

This work is the heart of the whole writing process adventure: revision.

Stephen King does all this too, very fast, much faster than I can; newspaper reporters are veritable blurs of light, they move through this process so fast. But it's the same process.

The writing process, then, is not just a blathering sloppiness and a lot of unfinished bits of fantasy floating about the already messy desks of young children. It is a celebration of each child, one avenue for the increasingly necessary building of self and of self-esteem in our children, as well as the vehicle for learning all the ins and outs of the language itself. That's what Donald Graves and others have done: they have given all of us, children and teachers, permission to help children be themselves in their learning.

Winter. Snow. Wet mittens. Smelly boot liners. Rules about snow.

We'd been making a set of rules about winter playground behavior. Finally, after much debate, we had our list, and it included the one school-imposed rule: no snowball throwing on the playground at recess. To make the children feel better, I said I wished it didn't have to be a rule: I liked to throw snowballs, too.

"You do?" exclaimed Cory, his seven-year-old eyes crinkled in disbelief. Various others snorted in agreement with him.

I read this in the circle, and as I read I realized I wanted to change the word *throw* in the first sentence to "play with," so I took my marker and drew a line through *throw* and wrote "play with" above it.

"Sure," I said, amused. "But don't worry, I know the rule around here, even if I don't like it."

Then it was time to start putting on all those boots and mittens for recess, and we left it. The next morning, however, when we were all working on our individual writings, I decided to write about my snowball habit. On a chart, where I often write, I put down this draft:

Snowballs

I love snowballs best when I get to throw them, too. I would much rather throw them than yell about them. When I go out to recess, it's my recess too so why can't I throw snowballs?? There is a rule, though, about it. It isn't fair to teachers, but it's a rule anyway. Teachers are supposed to obey the rules just like the kids do.

I read this in the circle, and as I read I realized I wanted to change the word *throw* in the first sentence to "play with," so I took my marker and drew a line through *throw* and wrote "play with" above it. "There, I revised it a little," I told them.

"Okay," said Cory, "but I don't really believe it."

That day the other second-grade teacher asked me to come to her class to show them how to go about revision. This class hadn't done much writing and she wanted to get them going. So I took that "Snowballs" chart into their room while my class was in music.

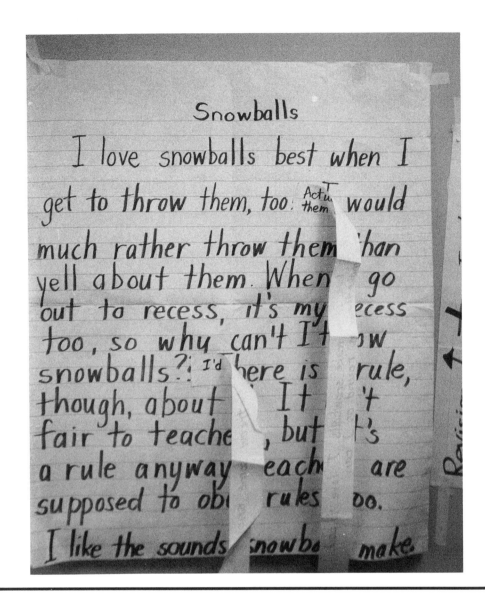

Snowballs

I love snowballs best when I get to throw them, too. Actu. them would much rather throw them 'han yell about them. When go out to recess, it's my ecess too, so why can't I t ow snowballs?: I'd here is rule, though, about It 't fair to teache , but t's a rule anyway each are supposed to ob rules oo. I like the sounds snowbo make.

"I want to read to you a little story I've written, and I'd like you to help me make it better," I told the second-graders. "Read along with me if you want to." And we read the chart aloud. After we finished I asked them what they liked about it. They tried to find something.

"It's nice," said Brandi, voicing the tepid majority opinion.

"I think it's kinda neat for a teacher to like snowballs," said Craig.

"Thanks," I replied. Craig had certainly given me a positive response. I waited, but no one else said anything. "Not very exciting, though, is it?" I continued, giving them permission to comment. "Is there anything you want to know more about, or anything that isn't clear to you?"

They considered this, looking sideways at each other and at their teacher, sitting noncommittally nearby.

"Well," said Kenny slowly (Kenny was Cory's older brother), "do you really like to throw snowballs? You're kidding, right?"

"No!" I told him. "I do like snowball throwing. Of course, what I *really* like to do is *make* snowballs—you know, pack snow together hard with my mittens on, making it as round and as hard and as packed as I can."

Lots of murmurs and nods greeted this confession.

"That's not in there," accused Saralyn.

"Yeah," echoed Tim. "I like that, too."

"Shall I put that into this story, Tim?" I asked him, smiling as with a wonderful new idea.

"Sure," said Tim.

And from the back row came a quiet voice speaking to the air, "Now she's going to have to copy it all over."

"I heard that!" I said. "And I'm not going to have to. Watch."

I reached over to the teacher's desk and picked up her scissors. I cut a strip off the bottom of the chart and wrote on it, "Actually what I like to do best is to pack them down as round and hard as I can." I took a piece of tape from my sleeve—I always have pieces of masking tape on my sleeve for just such emergencies—and taped the strip into place after ". . . than yell about them."

"There. Now let's read it together and see if it makes sense." They joined in chorally as we read the piece through again with the addition. "How's that? Better?"

"Yeah," they said. They tilted their heads to look at the strip, now dangling down from its taped end.

"Anything else?" I asked.

"Would you really throw snowballs at us if you could?" asked Jen.

"Weeeell, maybe," I answered. I lowered my voice to a big whisper and told them that there were a few teachers I'd like to try one on.

"Put that in, put that in!" came several voices; so I cut another strip and wrote on it, "I'd like to throw some at the other teachers." I attached it after ". . . snowballs??"

"Let's read it out loud again, and see if we like the revision," I directed them. It did sound better.

"Thanks, second grade, it sounds much more interesting, doesn't it? I have to get back to my class now. Do you know what you did here? You helped me to revise my story; you helped me decide what to add. Thanks!"

This procedure for a revision conference is so simple I will write it down:

Conference Procedure

First: The writer reads.

Next: Friends say, "I like the part . . . "

Next: Friends ask, "What . . . ?" or "Why . . . ?"

Next: The writer decides what to do.

Demonstrating a lesson like this, with writing of my own, however short, lets children know that I am serious about this idea of personally chosen topics. Demonstrating a lesson like this shows children how to begin to think about revising their own writing. First, of course, they have to have some writing of their own. This is the hardest part—for teachers.

We were not brought up ourselves, most of us teachers, to believe that we could be writers, not in the least as we encourage those students we now teach to believe they are and can be. Encouraging, believing that our students are and can be writers, is one of the trickiest things we teachers of writing as a process have been doing for the past ten years, and I find it fascinating that the success rate moves from the bottom up: that is, that more teachers of the lower grades are able to come to and then encourage this belief in their students than are the teachers of the highest grades. This paradox seems to be true, even though the older students, theoretically at least, should be the most able writers, most in command of the language. A part of the explanation for this little paradox, I sometimes think, is that lower grade teachers can suspend disbelief more readily or more intentionally than can high school teachers. We still believe in the tooth fairy, and of course there are those leprechauns on the playground that we almost catch every year . . . so it's not impossible for us to successfully pretend we are writers.

The changes that accompany seeing ourselves as writers, teachers and children alike, are profound. Remember when you were in third grade and your teacher said, on a Friday afternoon, "We've finished all our work for the week, so let's do some writing. Let's all write about our summer vacation!"

The name of the game in process writing is ownership; the child is the author of the whole thing and the teacher is not.

You remember this? Did you get the message that writing wasn't very important, not part of our "real" work in school? Did you realize what a lie she was telling, because she said "let's?" and then she didn't write at all, she went over to her desk and corrected math papers? "Let's" signals the first-person-plural imperative, which means that "we" are involved in the action of the command, we all, including her. She didn't write, though, another indication of how important this wasn't; she left you and your classmates to write about your summer vacation. Whether you wanted to or not, whether you had or would have a summer vacation or not, you had to write about it.

The real work of writing in school was penmanship practice.

Now, each student is expected, and encouraged, and taught by demonstration how to rework her ideas and to make changes and select new information or events, even if the thing feels like it might be finished at first. Everybody's writing is about something different, everybody talks about it while it's being written, it doesn't matter how long or short it is, and there is no "due on Friday" in it at all, nor any grades. Best penmanship plays a very minor role in writing process work.

Imagine.

The name of the game in process writing is ownership; the child is the author of the whole thing and the teacher is not. I make it a rule, for instance, never to carry a pen with me as I look over shoulders and listen to conferring friends and sit in on writing conferences, so that I will never be tempted to write on a child's paper.

Unfortunately it does seem at first glance to be linear, that is, prewriting, writing, revising, editing, all in a neat line, one before the other. There are teachers everywhere, I have met and argued with lots of them, especially in the intermediate grades, who have transplanted this little progression into the blocks of their plan books on four consecutive days, and it is how they "get the kids to write" now, instead of the old "Industries of New Mexico" and "If I were a Martian . . . " stuff. They still don't trust the kids to think of their own topics, they keep an intense eye on the spelling and penmanship throughout the week, they say, on Wednesday, "Now revise this," and they wonder why the stories are still short and the commitment lackluster. They are sticklers for margins, put grades and comments on the final drafts just as they used to, and wonder why everyone is so excited about this writing process stuff; it's just new wineskins for the old wine.

> **The soul of the thing is the ownership of the ideas, choosing the topic, writing about what is important or interesting to her, for that reason only, not because someone else suggested what to write about.**

I'm sorry. I think that everyone should have writing in the classroom, for its own sake in its own time as well as in and for and from other disciplines, but I think it is essential to start all those teachers down the writing process road simultaneously or even before, in in-service courses such as the Writing Project model. People who were not brought up to have confidence in themselves as writers, or who have not learned to have such confidence as grownups, cannot teach writing this way without training or, better, a conversion experience. It is asking much too much of them.

There is both heart and soul in writing process work, no matter how old or in what estate the writer finds herself. The soul of the thing is the ownership of the ideas, choosing the topic, writing about what is important or interesting to her, for that reason only, not because someone else suggested what to write about. Of all those thirty third-graders who were spuriously invited to join their teacher in writing about summer vacation, it is possible that two or three said to themselves, "Oh, goody, that's exactly what I want to do right this minute." As a teacher, I certainly don't want to count on that. Let people use their own power, revel in their own ideas, believe in themselves. Perhaps we could begin to substitute self-esteem for self-destruction on a planetary level, just by saying to our children, "Certainly! You can!"

Souls can be elusive at best and are easily smashed.

Revision has actually been part of our lives forever, although generally speaking we have not called it so. There is a lot of revision in speech, when we add another sentence to clarify, and in the expression "I mean" interpolated into conversation.

I truly believe that revision is easy, and that there are only three possibilities: +, −, and ~. A writer can add, take away, or change. I write these possibilities in signs to emphasize their simplicity, because many teachers feel daunted by the whole idea of revision. As we go along talking about it, though, light bulbs go on like popcorn because they can see that there is nothing new for them to learn, no new *whats* but only *hows* and *whens*.

Most young writers begin with adding, which is the easiest. While it is very true, it isn't especially successful to say to kids, "The easiest way to revise is to add more." Kids and grownups who are learning to be writers—that is students in school and students in in-service classes—are the same in that they all prefer to believe that they don't need to change their writing, that revision isn't anything they need or want to do. The curious difference between them is that the kids aren't interested in revision because they think their writing is perfectly okay, if not in fact perfect, the way it is; the teachers, generally, don't want to do anything more with it because it's so bad to begin with. The kids, you readily perceive, will be easier to teach.

> **First and last we make long division fascinating, and then we require it. We do the same with revision.**

To teach revision or not, by the way, is not a choice. Revision comes with the territory, just as division comes with the territory of math. If a child doesn't want to do long division, we usually don't say, "Oh, that's fine, it is complicated, you're right, why don't you just multiply for the rest of your life?" No. First and last we make long division fascinating, and then we require it. We do the same with revision.

Every morning on your board or your overhead put a boring sentence. It can be short, too, but it's best if it's boring. In first grade I use sentences such as "The dog ran." In third grade it might be "The women went hunting " or "The men went to the mall." The task is for students to expand this bare sentence before the pledge of allegiance begins; then we read a few of the children's expansions and discuss them. For the first few times, I'd put a caret or two or three to suggest where material could be added, such as after *The* and after *mall*. Keep track of these, collect them—not the papers themselves, but the sentences—and you can begin to classify them to use as examples of various grammatical constructions and labels, such as adjectives, prepositional phrases, adverbs, conjunctions, purpose clauses, compound/complex sentences. You all will begin to see that the words added after the *The* will tell what kinds of a _____ , and will be adjectives. The words added after the verb will tell how or where and will be adverbs or adverbial phrases. Some children enjoy classification and should have chances to do it. It, like everything else, is much more meaningful and fun (yes, grammar can be fun) when the stuff of it belongs to the people who are doing it. In a writing room, there is absolutely no need to have a grammar book or an English book for each child; use what they have to say and write as your texts and samples, and explore whatever you need to. Even the subjunctive will come up from time to time, even in first grade, if you feel pressed to notice it.

> **It is great fun to put a huge run-on sentence on the board from time to time, and invite revisers to play with it.**

Another little revision trick you can make part of the pre-pledge moment is the opposite of expanding: sentence combining. "It is cold today. It is rainy today" is a good beginning sample, and later perhaps "The girl walked out of the house. Then the girl walked down the street." The latter can go several ways, but some of those words will be taken away in any reworking.

Real work in the take-away department comes in weaning American English speakers from the words *and*, *very*, and *really*. Once again the distinction between oral and written language can be useful: there are a lot of things you can say in English that you don't write (*ain't* springs to mind) and the same is true of sentences. Run-on sentences are part of speech, not writing. Reading them aloud can be very helpful, because most sentences shouldn't require more than one breath to read aloud! Generally speaking, we take breaths at the punctuation. That's one of the reasons we have it. It is great fun to put a huge run-on sentence on the board from time to time, and invite revisers to play with it.

The best examples of revision come, of course, from the best writers. I sometimes say that you only need one book to teach everything about writing, and that book is *Charlotte's Web*. Nearly every page has a scene or a description that pulls the reader right into the text. The description of Mr. Zuckerman's swing in chapter 10 is brilliant on several counts, not least being the way the lengths of the phrases and sentences imitate the slowing and shortening of the arcs of the rope as it swings. Using this passage is one of the two ways I introduce revision with senses.

First, I read the passage aloud; then, depending on how raptly the children were listening, I read it again. "Now," I say, "what did E. B. White write in this part that you can see? What pictures did he put into your mind?"

Once they start coming, there are lots of answers to this question. The rope, the barn, the sky, the person swinging, the knot—all are shown in the passage. Then I ask about what he made us hear, of which the most obvious is the wind whistling, and there is always someone who hears the rope creaking, although White doesn't exactly mention it. Then I ask about the sense of touch, and nearly everyone has the feel of the rope and the rope seat, as well as, again, the wind.

"This author, E. B. White," I tell the students, "is one of the best. He thought about what he wanted his readers—that's us—to see, and hear, and feel, and made his words give us those senses. Now get out your own piece that you're working on right now, and see if there is a place where you could add some detail, maybe just one word, that will give your reader something to . . . touch. Look at your writing, add a word or a sentence that connects the reader to what you'd like your reader to feel."

This direction is easy and the students soon come up with something. Then I ask them to read the way they had it before and the way it is now, and some other child can identify the "touch" detail. You can do this with any of the senses (one at a time) and the writing is guaranteed to be improved, clearer, more interesting—all those subjective phrases that are useless as directions to student writers. "Make your writing more interesting" or even "Make your writing more descriptive" is practically impossible as a direction, not to mention how scary it can be. "Revise for the sense of smell" is much easier, much safer.

The other way to teach students to revise is by modeling a piece of your own writing for revision. I wrote this little beginning for a third grade:

> The girl went into the woods on the path nearest the house. Her little dog walked beside her, scattering the leaves with his tail. Suddenly it got dark and she knew it would rain soon. The dog was scared too. "What shall we do, Biscuit?" she asked. The dog whined his answer.

This group wanted the girl to have a name, first. "It's not fair, is it?" asked Levi, "for the dog to have a name and not the girl?" They agreed to name her Sally, after their student teacher.

"What could we do to add some hearing words to this story?"

"What could we do to add some hearing words to this story?" I asked. "What about this word *went* at the beginning? Could we change that so we could hear her walking? And what about the dog?"

"The dog is already making a noise, scattering leaves," said Annie practically. "But you could be moving them, too, as you walk, shuffling them."

"Okay," I agreed, crossing out *went* and putting in *shuffled*. There was more talk about this and when someone added *cautiously* there was general agreement. I wrote *thunder* in, too, because "they'd be able to hear it once it started."

This group was very bright, so we added a little taste and a little smell, too, so that before I sent them into their own folders to find a spot they could revise for a sense in their own work, the story looked like this:

> Sally was shuffling cautiously into the woods on the path nearest the house. Her little grayish-brown dog pranced beside her, scattering the leaves with his tail.
>
> Suddenly the clouds got dark and she knew it would rain soon. She could almost taste the raindrops. The dog was scared of thunder, too. "What shall we do, Biscuit?" she asked. She smelled the musty leaves. The dog whined his answer.

Several children shared their revisions, just as I shared mine.

It is also fun to send your students off into their reading, or the newspaper, or anywhere into their print environment, to find examples of their own of sensory detail, as well as sentences and bits of writing that cry out for revision, whether of the plus, taking away, or changing type. This, too, is ownership. This, too, continues to connect writing with reading. Another day you can ask them to be looking simply for language that is impossible to understand.

Government pronouncements, including memos from school administrators, and particularly announcements from airlines, are good sources for this. Circumlocutions, a nice word for double talk, can make people suspicious not only of each other, but of themselves. Why should anybody get away with something like "extinguish your smoking materials" for "put out your cigarettes"? In his book *A Writer Teaches Writing*, Donald Murray tells a story about President Franklin Delano Roosevelt: "When a World War II directive came across his desk, it read in part, 'In those establishments where suspension of labor is possible, direct those parties of management to the termination of the illumination.' He is reported to have crossed it out and written, 'In buildings where work may be stopped, tell the managers to turn out the lights.'"

If you know people in the Army, they will be excellent sources of over-cooked verbiage. Of course, if they are career Army people, they may not be able to spot it. It's fun to make up doublespeak, too, or have the kids do it, in pairs, one to be the circumlocutor and one to be the revisor. Again, this work will be done aloud as well as in writing, so the students will hear what their sentences sound like and begin to acquire a feel for what is mellifluous and accessible to the readers' inner ears as well as to their brains.

The simplest kinds of change are from the ordinary to the less ordinary, from the hackneyed to the unusual, from the cliché to the original, beginning with single words. Verbs usually come first here, in the changing department. How many times in a ten-page story can a writer use *said*? In a demonstration lesson on revision, I write a story with lots of saids and as it is read aloud and looked at, someone usually notices how dull that is. Then I can ask the students to look at a story of their own and find out how they have dealt with the problem. "Circle all your *saids*," I can tell them. (This is a whole-group lesson.) "Who has the most? Who has something different? What other words are possible today?" Then I can ask them to make a few changes right there, wherever in their own writings they want to, and I can make changes on my demo, as well.

Figurative language and metaphor are so exciting when they emerge, either from writing or from reading. Anybody who finds or writes some is given a moment to share it with all of us. I'll never forget Rob's description of the monster in his story "so ugly a mirror could break."

"Wow," exclaimed Justin when Rob read his piece about the monster. "That's really ugly!"

"That makes a picture," sang out Angela, quoting me—I'm always telling someone that their words make a picture.

"Yes, it does," I agree. "Should we save it somewhere, Rob?"

"It can go on the metaphor list, can't it?" asked Laura.

Aha, I thought. Yes. "Certainly," I told them. "Rob gets to write it."

It is in this way that we all learn what figurative language is, and about the differences between simile and metaphor and all those other bits that are usually reserved for a totally unrelated lesson in the middle of a selection of reading. Discovering these is the business of the members of the class, young and old. Very young children often speak and write in metaphor, and may as well know that's what they're doing. I may as well have a chance to applaud them and rejoice.

> **That's all I want to teach: that writers revise, these are some of the ways they do it, and you are writers too, so . . . there you are.**

Part of any discussion of run-on sentences will be the subject of sentence type and length. Looking at a paragraph in a book you are reading aloud is one way to get into this rather rarefied corner of revision. If I put on the board or the overhead, or on a ditto if that's legit for the group I'm working with, a paragraph of description by Laura Ingalls Wilder or Patricia McKissack or Eve Bunting or Roald Dahl or E. B. White, they know it's real. We read it aloud, listen to the flow, and try to determine why it flows so well. Then we count the words in each sentence, and find that they vary. Then we number the words in the sentences and find out how far into each one the verb comes, and if there is a comma, where; then we compare. Usually we find that the sentence types vary too, from straight subject-predicate, to introductory prepositional phrase, to dependent clause first, or last, or in the middle; there are simple sentences alternating with complex sentences, and sometimes there is a deliberate repetition of one type for emphasis. All these things the students can discover about the writing, and then, in a refrain, I ask them somewhat owlishly if they think the writer did it this way in his or her first draft. If I've done my teaching well, I'll get a chorus back: "No! The author revised!"

That's all I want to teach: that writers revise, these are some of the ways they do it, and you are writers too, so . . . there you are.

Revision, like everything else in this life, must be done in moderation. There is a story that Hemingway revised the ending to *For Whom the Bell Tolls* thirty-nine times. The story doesn't tell if he stopped revising because it was finally okay, or if his publisher came and grabbed it out of the typewriter. In my view, thirty-nine times is absurd. I would never do that to my own writing; at least I never have. In any case, what might be appropriate for Hemingway or for me would be annihilating for students. The issue of how much revision is a very real one for both teachers and students of every age in school.

In general, I take the minimalist position. Any addition, subtraction, or change, however small, constitutes a revision. In first grade, when a writer has done a story about her cat, the conference group gives her three ideas, such as the cat's name, where it sleeps, and how old it is. She may choose to add only the name, as in "I love my cat Smokey" instead of "I love my cat." For me, she has followed the basic rules of revision: 1. look at the piece again, with friends, and 2. make it different. Of course it may not be the most perfect story ever possible about Smokey, but the writer has used the rules for revision. That's all I ask. If I wanted to coach Pulitzer Prize winners I'd do my life differently.

> **In my opinion, a piece of writing done by an elementary school student doesn't need to be revised at all if it isn't going to be published.**

Then, as writers grow through the grades, they can do more. They can be expected to revise a piece or two twice, or three times; that's plenty, even for twelfth-graders, and only if those twelfth-graders have been writing for several years, owning and living with the writing process. In my opinion, a piece of writing done by an elementary school student doesn't need to be revised at all if it isn't going to be published. As the teacher, and as a writer, you can discuss the issue of whether or not to revise with them. I think that you should discuss with the students in every year not only what they perceive the process to be when they come to you—just to make sure you are speaking the same language—but also what everyone's expectations for the coming year will be. How much writing, for example, will you expect them to do, how many pieces will they publish per quarter, how will conferences be set up. Decide on these things together. There is no need for mystery any longer in education. Let's, truly, be in this together, and own the process in common.

Child-centeredness began with writing process, which was the first half of the current revolution in the teaching of language. With luck, the transformation to whole language will in turn become the first half of the teacher revolution, whose continuation will be the empowerment of teachers and the achievement by schools of their proper place in the society, that is, that school comes before everything else.

Notes: Revision

Revision is . . .

adding detail or information

taking away detail or information

changing something—arrangement of text, point of view, tense, details

Revision Conference Rules

1. Writer reads.
2. Friends say, "I like . . . "
3. Friends ask, "What about . . . ?" or "Why . . . ?"
4. Writer decides what to revise.

Revision conference procedure must be taught.

- Children can tell their friends what they like about the friend's writing as it is read in the daily sharing time, one or two "I likes . . . " per piece.

At conference, the teacher of children ages 7, 8, and 9:

- Writes the friends' suggestions on a sticky note.

- Puts the sticky note onto the child's writing so the group's suggestions for revision are available to the writer after the conference.

Older children can keep their own revision notes, either on a sticky note or on the piece itself.

Revision Lesson for Senses and Sensory Detail

- Listen to a piece of writing in which sensory detail is well done.

- Look at the piece of writing copied on a chart or overhead

- Find and underline in different ways things the reader can see, hear, touch, and so on, using different colors or different lines.

- Ask the children to suggest another detail for one sense.

- Write in the detail.

- Ask the children to go back to the piece they are currently working on and add one detail of one sense.

- Share the old and new parts.

This process can also be used with a piece of the teacher's writing—a different kind of power.

Revision Lesson for the Five Ws

- Listen to the reading of a beginning narrative you write on a chart or overhead.
- Find the "who" it is about.
- Find the "where" and "when.
- Ask if we readers know "what" is happening.
- Discuss if "why" is necessary at this point in the writing process.
- Add what's missing.

Other lessons, for endings, expanded middle, characterization, setting, denouement, even paragraphing and powerful verbs, can be handled in the same way.

10

Keeping Track

If I don't lead the children through their learning in an efficient and linear way, what do I do with my time? Well, the opposite of lead is follow, and that's what I do. The beautiful thing about it is that I don't have to both plan and record-keep; the one is the other. When I make notes on what has occurred in the connecting of Jeremy with math concepts, for example, or Tara with legible penmanship, or Jane with number facts, or Hong with understanding the water cycle, I know where they are. I know what I need to be sure those children can do in the coming days in order to extend themselves from where they are. I know what has to be available and also taught next, from the point of view of my agendas and also from theirs. My agenda for first grade includes, for example, addition but not multiplication (unless José or Bettina seems to be ready and enthralled); the water cycle *in toto*, but not the chemical composition of the various kinds of water from pure to polluted, at least partly because I don't understand that either; the alphabet and sound-symbol correspondence (unless Jake and Mai Tan don't learn in the auditory mode at all); reading and enjoying reading; writing and taking pride in writing; working together with people you like and with people who think differently; manners; and the ability to use time sensibly.

> I consider the anecdotal records of the children themselves as necessary and legitimate as those I keep myself.

Of course, keeping track of these things is in many cases subjective and can't usually fit into a neat classification from one to one hundred. Where my evaluation plan may differ from others is that I consider the anecdotal records of the children themselves as necessary and legitimate as those I keep myself. The fact that I may choose to show them mine and that they must show me theirs is a qualitative difference between adulthood and childhood.

> **I make a chart of all the children's names with big spaces next to the names, and I try to stick a few words into each space at some point in the day.**

It would be wonderful really if every classroom had two teachers in it all the time, one to teach and nudge and affirm and question, and the other to observe the children and keep track of what happens. Failing that, I make a chart of all the children's names with big spaces next to the names, and I try to stick a few words into each space at some point in the day. With fewer than twenty children, this might be just marginally possible; with more than twenty I have to subdivide them arbitrarily into three or more groups, and concentrate on the children of a different group each day. Of course Tiffany is bound to do something splendid on an "off" day, but if I'm awake I can catch it and make a note on her piece of the chart, and the chart has two advantages. One is that I don't have to shuffle through a lot of lists every minute I want to record something; the other, more necessary to the children, is that I deliberately concentrate on a different set of kids every day, which makes it likelier that at the end of the week I will not have blanks for anyone. There are always a few children who would slide completely through the cracks if I let them, or let myself let them.

The chart is also at my elbow when I look over writing books, read science logs, check rhyming ladders, admire entries in pattern books, hang paintings. If Vincent has recorded a five-variable inverted pattern that I didn't happen to see when it was laid out on his desk earlier, I note it. If Jana still uses *ch* for *dr*, I note it. All of these notes are accompanied by a date, naturally. These notes and these charts are my grade book, and are also the basis for the conversations I hope to have with everyone's parents at least twice in every year. Some schools, it seems, require parents to come to a conference with the teacher two times in the year and will not give the children their report cards or promotion cards until the parents come. Some places believe this requirement is an infringement of the parents' and the children's civil rights, and parents only come if they want to. That means I have seen Rocky's mother ten times and I have no idea what Lauren's folks look like. It is probably axiomatic to say that the Rockys of the world are doing fine and the Laurens are having trouble . . . .

These charts must be portable and easily replicable so I don't have to rebuild them every third day. It is easiest for me to make a master copy to xerox, with eight or ten children's names on it and spaces to write—can we ever get away from grids?—and keep them in a stiff-backed folder or notebook or, amazingly enough, a clipboard. It is certainly easiest for me, a right-brained, abstract-random, ENFP, to have something big enough not to lose and small enough to hold in my left hand while I am writing on it with my right.

Perhaps you think that I am going on and on about the mechanics of my keeping track, but I have too often given up in despair when I have used other systems. This one isn't foolproof either, because there is always and continually will be the problem of putting together all of the entries for Rocky and all of the ones for Tara, and so on and so on, so that I can see the progression of their learning and activities. Thank heavens for glue sticks! But then, too, the tedious act of cutting them apart and putting them together child by child is mindless enough, on the one hand, to do during a Sunday afternoon Patriots game, and also occasional enough to give me an opportunity to see patterns I might not see if I filed everyone in separate folders every day. Post-its, sticky notes, blank labels have begun to revolutionize this task for me, as they have for moving plans around in the plan book.

Another way to do this keeping track stuff I had high hopes for one year was an apron with two pockets, one for pencils and one for small, three-by-five cards. Moving through her day, observing and challenging and helping her second-graders, my colleague Geri pulls a card out of her pocket and makes an entry about whatever has caught her eye—that five-variable inverted pattern, for example, or the fact that Andrew has successfully moved from one activity to another without murdering anyone on the way, or a really carefully drawn illustration of Nate the Great by the usually slapdash Malinda. Then after school she reads them all and files them in a big card file box that has a tab for each child.

As I say, I thought highly of this idea and even made myself a very simple apron to go on with; but I found that there were days when I forgot I had it on; and after a few weeks I discovered I had many many entries in the file box for several students and none for some of the others; that discovery made me decide that I couldn't rely on myself to notice everyone every day without making a list. So for a while I had seven cards in my apron pocket every day, with certain children already chosen for that day's observation. But then—you have probably already figured this out—I couldn't remember which children I was planning to focus on that day and had to fish all the cards out of my pocket to see who was in there on any given day. I lost a lot of minutes looking into my pocket.

Another way that worked for quite a while was a notebook into which I wrote whatever I had to say and whatever funny stories and impotent frustrations had passed by that day. The entries became scantier as the year wound down, but I usually did a page or two at least, and on especially angry or happy days as many as five. In the long run, with these notebooks, I learned more about myself as a teacher than about what the children were learning, and it wasn't doing what I wanted my system to do.

Somewhere in there I had a brief affair with electronics: I was given a portable tape recorder, and I kept it on my desk so that every time I saw something I wanted to keep track of or remember I could just pick it up and talk to it, and when a side was full I could transcribe it. Surprisingly, I wasn't always able to find it, and the oddest thing was that I interrupted an event more by talking to the tape than I would have by writing about it; it was a continual fascination for some children. All-in-all the tape method was far more intrusive than I had expected.

> **"Read" is of course a very relative term with primary children, and I have embraced with the greatest delight Marie Clay's expression "reading-like behavior."**

When I first began to do nonbasal reading and nearly had to swear my life in blood to be allowed to do it at all it was even more important to know what books the children read and how well they read them. "Read" is of course a very relative term with primary children, and I have embraced with the greatest delight Marie Clay's expression "reading-like behavior." It comes before word-for-word reading, also a pleasantly self-evident label, and means what Eric is doing when he tells you what is going on in the pictures, or when Sharon holds the book right-side-up and turns the pages in the right direction one by one, talking the story at you.

So when I meet with the children individually and listen to what they have to say about the books they have been working on during their morning's work, I use a big looseleaf notebook in which I have a tab for each child and pages of "_____'s Reading Record." There is room on this roster for the date, the name of the book or story and its author, and a small space for me to check whether Homan or Marion demonstrated literal recall or inferential comprehension as we talked over the reading. There is a largish place for me to write down the unforgettable things the children say as they discuss literature with me. That's the most fun part. I also note if they are "really" reading or doing the r-l-b, and if so, how. Sounds like a lot? Not when I have three or four—no more—uninterrupted minutes with Billy and with Beth and with Kial and with Rachel every four or five days.

One year, in the days when I used volunteers a lot because not everybody's mother was working yet, there was an epidemic about *The Teeny Tiny Woman*. I don't remember which version it was, although I know it wasn't the Tomie dePaola one, which wasn't published yet. Anyway, my volunteer on

Thursdays was Fran, mother of Matthew, and part of her morning's work was to listen to children read to get cards added to their Reading Ribbons. (I'll explain about them in a minute.) At the end of one Thursday morning she was helping me get everyone on the road to lunch, and I said, as always, "Thanks for coming today, you were a big help," and she said, "Well, I don't know if I can take another day like this one. You may have to look for another Thursday person."

"What happened?" I asked anxiously.

She sighed, with an unsmiling and cross face. "I'll come back on one condition," she said sternly.

"Tell me," I said anxiously.

"That you hide *The Teeny Tiny Woman* on Thursdays." Twinkles broke through. "Do you know how many times I had to listen to the Teeny Tiny Woman's troubles today?" she went on, rolling her eyes as we all started the long trek to the lunchroom.

"I give up," I said happily.

"I listened to that book *nineteen* times!!"

"No!" I said, astonished. "That's amazing."

"Amazing, ha!" replied Fran. "If I have to hear 'Give Me My Bone!' *one more time*, I will scream, too!!"

"Okay, okay," I promised. "On your next day I'll hide it. Or, look at it this way, Fran, if nineteen of them have already read it to you, there are only twelve more . . . "

"Aaaaghh!" said Fran, and we both laughed.

These reading ribbons Fran was working on are my version of bookworms, and I like them because they involve no expense or use of paper. The ribbons themselves are the long fat ones that come on fancy flower arrangements, and which are no good to use as ribbons again because they almost invariably have a few water spots in addition to the squinches and twists in the ribbon itself from being tied in elaborate bows. I take them home and iron them as flat as they will get and cut them into three foot lengths, write the children's names on the ends, and have a multicolored hanging record of each child's extra reading. The only rule about what you can read for a ribbon entry is that you can't read the same book, or the same part of a book, twice.

I use volunteers and older kids for this listening. If it's a long book, such as *The Fantastic Mr. Fox* or *Bread and Jam for Frances*, not to mention *The Lion, the Witch, and the Wardrobe* or *Misty of Chincoteague*, the reader has to choose a part or a chapter, five or six pages, to read to the listener. Then the child can choose to put just that chapter's name on the ribbon, or the whole book. It's possible to have a whole section of ribbon, six or eight entries, all from the

At the end of the year I also go through my reading records and type out a list of the books each child has read with me for the next teacher.

same book. Each entry, by the way, is the title written on a small piece of scrap paper the width of the ribbon and about an inch long. Simple. These are stapled to the ribbon.

That's how I keep track, or rather the kids, the volunteers, and I keep track, of what the children are reading on their own. The children who have a ribbon with entries on it get a prize in June (guess what). At the end of the year I also go through my reading records and type out a list of the books each child has read with me for the next teacher.

Writing needs to be kept track of, too. When I am Doing Words, I write down the Words a child gets, from the first day on through the beginning of Movement IV. I cross out the Words I have to take away; by keeping this list up to date I have a good visible touchstone to add to my gut feeling for how ready each one is to move to the next movement. Many people, oddly enough many administrators among them, aren't content with mere beliefs and gut feelings when describing the progress children make in school, so I find it helpful to have these backup tangible checklists and records and ribbons and picture logs and buildings and other samples of work.

As children in first grade become daily writers and get into revision and editing, I staple a recording sheet to the inside of the writing folders. It's so simple it's embarrassing and the beauty of it is that it serves at least three utterly different purposes. It's called (in big letters across the top, preferably with an exclamation point at the end), "What _____ can do as a writer!" Down the left side are simply numbers, as many as will fit—usually 8 or 9—and a space for dates going down the right side. This sheet, though perhaps in more sophisticated Macintosh graphics for the later grades, is equally useful all the way up the grades.

The first purpose is, of course, simply laudatory: Look what you can do! Secondly, this checklist is for self-editing. Many things on this list that have to do with the structure of writing and the inflections of the language are now the writer's responsibility. Robin, for example, is expected to check her work for periods at the ends of sentences; Sara can use, and therefore must use, commas in a series where necessary; Ahmed, in third grade, understands about paragraphing and so will not bring an unparagraphed piece to an editing conference with his teacher. Chuck has mastered the difference between *two* and *too*, so he must use them correctly before I see the writing;

Antonio's names must all have capitals. The students or I can add to these lists, but neither can add something unilaterally. For the least able ones there are still writing accomplishments worthy of praise, such as making beautiful letters, even single letters, frontward; Billy makes beautiful *B*s and *M*s; Jolene's letters are always on the lines; Carmella remembers to put the spaces between her words now. The third thing this chart is good for, of course, is for me to show parents and others what growth is happening in _____'s writing.

I talk each item over with the writer in question before I put it down, so that he or she will get a small burst of strokes, and so that they will know it's there, purposes one and two above.

Nicholas was a teeny tiny bit surer than I was that he could deal correctly with his language, right from the start. One day he absorbed commas, because they are, after all, fun to make and we had had a bunch of them in a chart we'd done the day before. In his writing that day was the sentence, "He had a pistol, a Uzi, and a knife."

"Look, Mrs. Johnson," he said importantly—Nicholas always spoke importantly—"I've put commas in here. See? To separate these weapons he has, see? So the reader won't think a pistol and the Uzi are the same thing."

> **I took his folder and on the "What Nicholas can do" sheet I made a comma lightly with my pencil and slanted out seven spokes from it.**

"Which of course they aren't," I agreed, although guns are not as important to me as to Nicholas. "That's certainly a help to your reader."

"So will you put it on my list?" he asked.

"Well, no, I don't think so, not today, Nicholas. Would that be fair, do you think? This is your first day for commas."

"Yeah, but I'll always do them now," he said earnestly. "I like them!"

I pondered. He had liked exclamation points, too, a few months ago, and they were everywhere for a while until he calmed down.

"How old are you?" I asked.

He gave me a look. "Oh, no, not that old thing," he said.

"Yes, that old thing," I repeated, grinning, but more determined on my course now that he was putting down my most old faithful trick.

He sighed. "I'm seven, you know I'm seven. Okay, okay."

I took his folder and on the "What Nicholas can do" sheet I made a comma lightly with my pencil and slanted out seven spokes from it. "There.

Now you used commas today, so I'll circle one of these spokes, and when they're all circled we'll write 'Nicholas can do commas in a series,' and I'm sure you'll be the first one." I circled one as I spoke. "How's that?"

"Well, that's not fair at all!" he exclaimed. "Look at this story! See?" He flipped papers until I was looking again at the pistol and the knife stuff. "Two commas today, see? I used two." He pointed indignantly at the paper.

I burst out laughing. I did love Nicholas. I circled another spoke around his big comma. "You sure did, and I'm impressed."

Satisfied at last, he went about his business.

As I describe these ways I have used to keep records of what kids do as readers and writers, it occurs to me that it may not be clear how I know what to look for. Why doesn't paragraphing come before commas? When and how does Ahmed learn about paragraphing? Nicholas was shown about commas in a chart story; why didn't everybody get it?

> **Take the child where she is and take her as far as she can go. And him, of course.**

I have in my head a long and tortuous list as well as a wide and bottomless sea of information about what children of different ages can do, like to do, and ought to do. Many years ago I began building this subconscious list of expectations when I first began my life as a teacher. Since then I have seen and worked with and listened to so many children and so many teachers that I have begun to learn what to expect, listen for, and say next.

There are some advantages to getting older.

Take the child where she is and take her as far as she can go. And him, of course. To me this means figure out what any child, every child, needs next in the context of the grade and make sure it's presented in ways he or she can grasp, ways that fit into this one's context or onto that one's scaffolding.

I do believe in asking the children to report on their work. This request can be made in any grade, and should be. It's all very well to say that they can make their own path through learning, but what do the children pass in to be checked? Because I am so oriented to writing, it is a *sine qua non* in any classroom for which I am responsible that each child has a writing book or folder and writes in it every day. These writings are stories or reports or journalings or descriptions or whatever someone wants to write, and are the basis for the revisions and publications the children do. They also provide me with a lot of clues about who needs to be taught what.

Writing is also a way to report on reading. I ask the children to keep a log of what they read every day, in a notebook set aside for that purpose. On one or two days the "log" is in the form of a dialogue with a partner about the books that each one read that day. On another day the child may choose to do a picture log instead, recording the "best part" of the book in a drawing, with its name and the date. In the written reading log there is a progression, from a few words with a big drawing to a lot of words with no drawing. I look these logs over every day; since there is a lot of invented spelling and language in them, they are even more valuable to me for diagnostic use. The writings I find the most fun in the early grades are those that are kept in response to a science or history or social science study. And all this evaluating and record keeping is really the raw material of planning. Generally speaking, the line between planning and evaluating blurs as less and less frontal pour-it-in teaching is done, and more and more of the time, the children are working and playing their way to learning in centers and small groups and at varying rates. Planning truly becomes a continuing process, and what the children have done leads us all into what we will do next.

> **I ask the children to keep a log of what they read every day, in a notebook set aside for that purpose.**

It may seem obvious to say, but I will say anyway, that the more child centered the classroom is, the more *ad hoc* work will probably be done, and the less preplanning will ever bear fruit. A fully inscribed grid of a plan book not only presupposes but requires a teacher-centric classroom where the suggestions and questions and interests of students must often be met with "Perhaps we can talk about that tomorrow" or "I'm afraid we don't have time to do that" or "No."

When you are in a child-centered, language-filled room, the children have agendas of their own and follow them with nudges from you, beside and behind, and there are as many paths as there are children.

In the ambience of the classroom, then, the responsibility for checking up on what the students have accomplished is theirs as well as mine. Among the many many things we are trying to provide for the children of these very unsettled times is a sense of accomplishment and self-esteem, as well as a little control over their environment. That's why I believe in giving to the children as much power as they can possibly handle, and then just a little more, so that they will learn how to be in charge of themselves and make decisions about what affects them. There are rules and consequences; you have to read, you have to write, you have to report about these activities or share them with someone and that someone can be me, the teacher.

We need always to evaluate a student in terms of that student's learning alone.

In my ideal classes at any and all levels of schooling, I know what the curriculum goals are for the year, the school, and the district, and I set out some content that fascinates me first, then, with the children, see where we can take it to satisfy as many of their related interests and puzzles as we can. As we go along, when we bump into something that we're "supposed" to "cover," we highlight it as long as we need to. This way I get to model excitement about learning, they get to do work in areas that intrigue them and, in doing so, become intrigued by learning, and the district gets its objectives taught. I never will, however, guarantee that learning occurs because teaching does—it's not a causal relationship. We need always to evaluate a student in terms of that student's learning alone.

"Oh, look," said Karla in surprise one winter morning, as we looked through her writing portfolio. "Here's my unicorn picture I made in kindergarten. I remember this. Why is it in my folder?"

"Well, Karla, you actually did that this year," I said. "See the date in the corner there?"

"9 slash 27," Karla read. "When was that? What's *9* stand for?"

"September," I said. "Just at the beginning of first grade."

Karla looked at the unicorn picture, noticing the letters that straggled across the upper right side of the paper. "*K, N, L, K, I*" she read, her voice deeply puzzled. "I wonder what that means," she mused.

I had been in first grade for fifteen years longer than Karla had, so I translated for her. "I think you wrote 'I like unicorns' there," I told her.

Karla looked at me, to see if I was teasing; then she looked back at her September picture. "Boy," she said emphatically. "I sure can write better now!"

The best thing about portfolio assessment for me the teacher is that I can look at a child's portfolio at any time during the year and see progress. I can feel that I have been a factor in the child's development as a writer, or as an artist, or as a reader, or as whatever I keep portfolio records about. In the middle of winter it is a wonderful thing to be able to feel that you've had some meaning in the lives of your students.

But even more important than how I come to feel about myself, exponentially more important, in fact, is how the students come to feel about themselves when they, too, can look at their growth. Karla's unicorn writing clearly told her how much she had grown.

How well the children—and you—can see their growth depends on how much latitude, practice, and trust your classroom provides. The writing portfolio, compiled by the student with consultations with the teacher, reflects a daily writing program whose content and process empower the student. The general picture of writing time can remain essentially unchanged from first to eighth grade, or any combination of grades in a self-contained or language arts–block setting. I have tried to describe it in chapters 8 and 9. On any given day there will be children talking over their writing in ones and twos as well as in groups, writing, revising, editing, publishing, and probably a few reading or researching, as well. These young writers work in writing conference groups on a weekly basis (or more often), learning through their own writing and that of others what "works" in writing.

Periodically—weekly at least, and daily is better—it is important to read aloud to the class a passage or a book that illustrates good writing, talk about it, perhaps even practice it, so that by the beginning of November you can begin to have giant discussions of what makes good writing good. You can teach them to "score" their own pieces, holistically and analytically if that will also help them to identify "what works."

What we need constantly to be doing, we teachers, is the difficult task of helping children to see a clear picture of who they are and what they can do, and the even more difficult task, to believe in themselves.

What we need constantly to be doing, we teachers, is the difficult task of helping children to see a clear picture of who they are and what they can do, and the even more difficult task, to believe in themselves. "To be nobody but yourself in a world which is doing its best, night and day, to make you like everybody else," said e.e. cummings, "is to fight the hardest battle any human being can fight; and never stop fighting." The point of using portfolios as evaluation is to help the student evaluate him- or herself. This is the ideal place to collect evidence of learning, to teach self-evaluation and self-esteem and self-knowledge. After all, what we must send out from our schools is a group of humans who know their own worth, know how to learn, and know the value of others as well. One of the most unfortunate features of traditional teacher-centered schools and classrooms is the mystery of the teacher's gradebook; underlying that is the absurd understanding that everything every child does can be reduced to a number or a letter grade, and that only the teacher has the code of how the child's work can be so translated.

Not that you will be able to know, any more than you ever did, exactly what the child is thinking. Linda Rief, of Oyster River Middle School in Durham, New Hampshire, believes in portfolios as self-assessment. Her students learn to think for themselves and to carry out their own direction in reading and writing; they also learn to know when they need help and how to get it. Linda still can't read minds: "You have to trust that they know a lot they don't tell you, and they need to be able to trust you tremendously so that they will be able to tell what they know."

What do you think of this piece? What do you like about it? Are there any questions you have about it? Do you think you'll work on it again sometime?

The use of portfolios can be for a single class, or for a whole school. Ideally, a portfolio can follow a child throughout elementary school, as a continuing record of accomplishment in which she or he has actively participated. Not only have the children been intimately involved in the process of producing the works in a portfolio, they have been one of two instruments, the other being the teacher, in choosing what is in it for six years in a row. Big three-ring binders are good for portfolios.

Karla's is typical of the growth of first-graders: phenomenal. The portfolio that contains the transition from picture-and-scribble or picture-and-letter labels to connected text in standard English and penmanship is the most exciting one of all to me. The writer's portfolio shows very clearly all the aspects of language use and when they became automatic for the student. I always save the very first piece of paper the child has decorated with picture and print combinations on the first day of school, and arbitrarily another something at the beginning of each month the children are in school, so my "choice" of pieces is never fewer than eleven. Then along about Thanksgiving (with Karla's class I didn't get to it until closer to Christmas), I spend time with each child and his or her writing folder, sorting through the pieces that have been begun, revised, or completed and published, asking the child to talk about them in conference terms:

What do you think of this piece?

What do you like about it?

Are there any questions you have about it?

Do you think you'll work on it again sometime?

What I listen for in the answers is fire. Another way to say it is that the child will show a commitment—Amanda always bounces on the chair, which is her sign of commitment to her writing. It may also come in their language—"I really *really* like this because . . . " For example, a third- or fourth-grader will be able to say, "I'm choosing this because my dialogue is really lifelike—this is my best dialogue ever." The second-grader is more likely to say, "I like the way I made them talk to each other in this story."

After this small discussion, the child chooses a piece to go in the portfolio, and it is carefully labeled: "'The Monster and the Piano,' October 1989, published"; "'My Cats,' May 1993, first draft."

Ideally this pride-making conference will happen four times a year, before each ranking period. Sometimes I actually do make four times, but I think three is just as good. Often the physical item in the portfolio is a photocopy of the original piece, unless the art work *is* the piece. Then there is usually an argument about whether the thing goes home—after an appropriate period on display—or not.

At the end of the year, the child chooses, out of all the pieces now in the portfolio, the most wonderful ones. A couple may be removed at this point, but that's not obligatory. I then remove, with the child's approval, all the monthly entries. Sometimes I send them home, sometimes I save them, sometimes I use them as samples to show other children how to be critical of a piece of writing not their own.

Contrary to what the basal system teaches, phonics is not a reading skill but a writing skill, as is paragraphing.

The same portfolio can be used for reading records as well, but it's pretty unwieldy, so I may have at least two portfolios going at the same time. Although we don't separate reading from writing, philosophically, we teachers still have to cope with the residue of fifty years of the basal-reader system of separating language unnaturally into tiny bits and arbitrarily labeling some of them "writing skills" and some of them "reading skills." Contrary to what the basal system teaches, phonics is not a reading skill but a writing skill, as is paragraphing. Comprehension, as Frank Smith (1985) so rightly says, isn't a reading skill at all; it *is* reading. A writing portfolio, then, may also hold checklists of such things as all the beginning consonant blends the child can identify and other similar holdovers.

In a reading portfolio I like to keep lists of what a child reads alone, what he reads with me individually, what he reads in small literature groups, and whatever else he is reading. There will be monthly samples of the child's responses to his reading in the form of log entries, book reviews, or entries in a daily response log kept with a classmate. Sometimes it's appropriate to put in the folder a project, or its description at least, if the child doesn't mind. (The way we kept the giant papier-mâché peaches—a group project once, individual ones other times—in the portfolio was by photographing them.) A child can also choose to take some items out of the folder. Nearly every teacher who keeps reading portfolios seems to do it the same way, from first grade to eighth, so I conclude that either this is a good idea, or that the teachers I talk to are all at my same stage of development!

The big question: How do you grade them and the work inside them? Or do you? How can we teach responsibility if we hedge every tiny move with an external judgment call? What is the relationship between taking responsibility for working through the process of writing and working through the process of life?

I find it impossible, personally, and I don't try, to grade writing as an aesthetic product. I grade the process. If the child has done the required work, the required revisions and editings and publishings and conferences, that child gets an *A* from me, or a plus, or an *S*, or whatever pseudonyms grades have this year. If the child has done most of it, say three-quarters of what should have been done, that child gets a *C*, or whatever is passing. Any other combination is a failure—but much more for me than for the child.

My stated goal or requirement for primary children is that they each take one piece of writing through the process, with conferences for revision and several kinds of editing (self-, peer-, teacher-), to publication, once a quarter. In second grade, *only if it is their second year of writing*, I would require two pieces, and increase every year until the total is four. That's plenty for anyone!

When I look at Amanda's writing, writing about a subject she is fascinated by for some reason, I can find out nearly anything I need to know about where she is with language. I can find it out in context, for the language she uses is loaded with meaning. I can find it out sitting with Amanda, in an editing session or a portfolio review, or I can do it alone, looking at her papers and notes and logs and stuff. Either she can spell *doesn't* or she can't; either she uses periods consistently or not; either she starts words with their correct sounds as she writes or she doesn't. Either she reads, as opposed to "reads," or she doesn't. I know what direction to go in teaching her.

Look at all that I can learn about Amanda and what she has learned and still needs to learn from simply comparing two pieces of her writing. She wrote the following on October 30:

> Im FL DAaW tR SAER
> I WRZ SER IDE
> DEE LREC ET
> my mom a DaD CAm
> REN DRT SER a

(I'm falling downstairs. It was scary. I didn't like it. My mom and dad came running downstairs and). On May 23 she wrote the following:

> 5/23
> My mom never does't any thing with me. She duas things with her sisters but not me. I gas she does't love me. My Dad duseit do any thing with me. Know buty duas any thing with me. My mom did not do any thing with me. My Dad had a trip. My sister was at Katy's. I did not have any fun.

There is no need to do any standardized test, out of context, outside of Amanda's life. The standardized tests (or national and state assessments or educational progress reports or whatever they may be called) we still support are a black hole of education not only because of what these tests do to Amanda, although nothing Amanda experiences in such testing is good, supportive, or child centered in any way at all. The destructiveness of these tests is in what they say to teachers: "You are not to be trusted to know what the children in your charge can do. You are not intelligent enough to draw conclusions about the performance of children, and, really, you probably aren't teaching very well anyway."

The movement toward thorough portfolio evaluation of children, especially with their opinions included in the evaluation, may bring about the beginning of the end of testing, of both children and teachers.

Notes: Keeping Track

It's essential to know how and what children are working on and learning, and equally essential to have a balance of anecdotal and linear values and records. It is also essential to have student evaluations and plans as well as teacher evaluations and plans for work in language.

For writing, keep:
- anecdotal records
- lists for each student of what Words they have had and which ones, if any, they have lost through Movement III
- checklists of what each child is doing in writing time every day
- goal-setting papers done with each child periodically
- what _____ can do as a writer!

- lists of publications, by genre, of the class
- lists on the children's writing folders of pieces they have begun
- portfolios

For reading, keep:

- anecdotal records, stories of how Jonathan "could read it if he knew what it was about," and Kelli's discovery that all of the Carle books she'd read so far were about animals (the beginnings of understanding what style is)
- reading records, lists of what each child is reading to you
- reading ribbons, sets of "extra" books read to a volunteer
- reading response logs, books read in SSR, two to four times a week
- goal setting papers done with each child periodically

Student records can also include:

- math investigations log
- scientific observation booklets
- evaluations of themes or group work
- products of theme or group work, real and photographed

Teacher records can also include:

- anecdotal stories about particular children's conversations, events, and projects
- charts of student learning objectives
- notebook (or cards or a clipboard) and sticky notes
- journal

In the writing portfolio:

- Keep a copy of whatever each child is writing at the first of each month in a set of folders or boxes in which everything is dated and labeled.
- Put into this file any other writings the child wants to stop work on or asks to have in it.
- Every few months, sit down with each child and go over the contents of the portfolio.
- Ask, What do you like about this piece? What questions do you have about it? What do you want to do with it? What makes this piece important for you?

In the math portfolio:

- teacher's record and photo of structures, patterns, and so on
- child's choice from all of one kind of work (geoboards, patterns, and so on)
- child's and teacher's selections from the math investigations log

In the science and social studies portfolio, keep:

- reports and observations the child and teacher agree are special
- photos of special projects (dioramas, constructions, experiments, and so on)

Portfolios are better for children and teachers than testing because:

- A fill-in-the-blanks or circles format is alien to classroom work.
- Testing grows numbers, not people.
- Portfolios are part of the world outside of school. Employers want to know "What can you do?" not "What percentile are you on?"
- Children can see and take pride in themselves through portfolios.

Teachers can see and take pride in their work, too.

11

Grammar as You Go

On a particular December day, an ordinary December day, the children were writing as usual the long and short, fantasy and reporting, simple and complicated writings they wrote every day. A tremendous variety, twenty-nine different topics—thirty counting mine—wafted through the air and the brains around the room. Everyone was busy writing on something that each one had thought of and wanted to write.

The energy and concentration were tremendous, too.

At 9:45 we all put down our pencils and brought our writing folders to the carpeted circle on the floor. As the students each read the writing of that day, I took notes on their uses of the past tense verb ending *-ed*.

"The six boys were trapped in the space ship." Rob read his writing, a continuation of a story he'd been working on every day for the past week.

> **The *AAAAA* got attention from everyone. "How did you write that?" I asked, and Rob showed the page of his book.**

"'What do we do now? asked Matt. Let's stay calm said Jason. OK said John. I'm scared said Rob. He ran into the cockpit, screaming AAAAA. He bumped a button near the window. The ship moved."

The *AAAAA* got attention from everyone. "How did you write that?" I asked, and Rob showed the page of his book.

"I choose Bonnie," he said, and Bonnie read hers, a beginning.

"Once upon a time there was a puppy. His name was Jeremy. He crawled over to his mother. The mother took his neck in her teeth. So she could carry him to the box."

Bonnie chose Cindy, and the reading/choosing the next reader procedure continued. Toward the end of the reading time Jason read the current part of his story:

"Jeffrey and Melinda were inside the strange house when it began to rain. Melinda was scared. I'm scared, she cried. She wanted to go outside. Jeffrey found a candle and a match."

"Aah! And what's he going to do with that match!?" I asked.

"You'll have to wait until tomorrow," said Jason, shutting his book. "I'm all done!"

And we were all done, too, with reading. It was recess, then, and everybody put away writing folders and stories and pencils and took off for the playground.

Later that morning—or perhaps it was the next morning—after silent reading, I pulled the class together for a grammar lesson.

"Look at these sentences, please, and tell me what they all have." I wrote on the board, "Rob bumped a button." "This is from Rob's story yesterday," I told them. "Rob, would you read this, please?"

> ## "Look at these sentences, please, and tell me what they all have."

Rob did, and I wrote another one. "Bonnie, would you read this?"

"He crawled over to his mother," read Bonnie, a sentence from her story about the puppy.

"And Jason, would you read this?" I asked, writing one more.

"She wanted to go outside," read Jason.

"Thanks," I said.

All three of these sentences were now printed on the chalkboard. We read all three of them out loud, with the authors leading the choral reading; then I asked the class what was the same about these three sentences.

Hands shot up. We had done this kind of thing often enough! "They all have an -*ed* word," came the answer.

"That's what I noticed, too," I said. "Who can come up here and put a line under the word with -*ed* in Jason's sentence?"

So all the verbs in question got underlined. Then I asked, "What is the base word in *bumped*? What is it without the -*ed*?"

I called on someone to tell me, to spell it while I wrote it to the left of Rob's sentence. The other two were done the same way. Then I said, conspiratorially, "Now watch carefully . . . " and I erased the three past tense verbs from the sentences. The board now looked like this:

bump Rob _____ a button.

crawl He _____ over to his mother.

want She _____ to go outside.

It is not okay for Americans to be ignorant of the structure of the English language.

From this point the lesson could go several ways. I could ask for other volunteers to fill in the blanks with the correct words, being careful to use different children from those who had already helped and also different children from those who had done this before. I could leave it on the board to be copied as seatwork during the small-groups-meeting-with-me part of the morning, before lunch. I could put it onto a ditto and use it for paper seatwork or homework. I could put it on a laminated chart paper to be completed by a particular group during the time for centers and Words the next day. I could ask the children to find three words like these in whatever they are reading and add them to the chalkboard (this is the most difficult one, since many stories for early readers are written in present tense). Or, since it seemed to be fairly easy for nearly everyone, I could forget all about it.

The beauty of this system is that the whole class is acquainted with these little bits of text, since they have heard them read as part of the stories written by Rob, Bonnie, and Jason. This familiarity gives both the sentences and the point of grammar an interest value which a grammar book can never give. There is ownership and connection, without which learning is less likely.

When I use the word *grammar,* as in the title of this chapter, it is a kind of shorthand, a generic word, an all-inclusive label for the elements of our language that have traditionally been presented to children, all children at all ages and grades, in fragments. From forever, there has been an "English" book, or a grammar book, in the desks of all children, sometimes from grade one up. There is no connection to my children in these books, nor in the others that have stuffed children's desks: penmanship; spelling; phonics; even, or especially, the "reading" workbook designed to fragment even further the already-fractured story in the meaningless basal.

When I suggest that the teacher and the class can do "grammar as you go," I mean all of those elements. I believe that they can all be included as offshoots of and part of the daily writing time.

When a child is engaged in her own writing, . . . the focus is quite powerful.

Not only can they be included, they must. It is not okay for Americans to be ignorant of the structure of the English language, especially as they are using it in school. It is also not okay, and what's more doesn't work in our present culture, to expect children to be interested in external text and unconnected sentences enough to learn anything from them. One of the (many and unfortunate) legacies of television is that children won't give their attention to anything that doesn't interest them. Not for your sake, not for mine. When a child is engaged in her own writing, however, the focus is quite powerful. Her energy for her own writing is high and full of commitment. Channel that power, that energy, into the study of a point of letter formation, verb inflection, apostrophes, punctuation, sentence structure—any "grammar" point—and she will not even realize that it's a lesson, so connected is she by the ownership of her own or her classmates' writing.

Language is not fragments strung together at random. Nor do you write a story or an essay by subdividing the language grammatically. You don't write down first all the nouns, then all the commas, then all the plural endings, then the verbs . . . that's ludicrous. But teaching the language in bits, out of any context, is just as ludicrous.

English is just about the richest and most complicated and fascinating language humans have yet come up with. Share that with children. Let them be amazed and fascinated—and frustrated—by their own language. Don't try to convince them that the rules of English spelling and phonics make sense; they don't. Even the easy ones, such as "drop the final *e* before you add *ing*" (whether you use magic dust or not), are only true most of the time. Remember *canoeing!*

> **"Play Doh is sticky," I repeated, marker in hand. "Who can tell me how to start this sentence? Steve?"**

In another class one day, we charted "discoveries" students had made during the morning. As always, I asked various children to help me spell as I wrote on the chart. Kim started us off with her discovery: "Play Doh is sticky but it's fun," she said.

"Play Doh is sticky," I repeated, marker in hand. "Who can tell me how to start this sentence? Steve?"

"Capital *P*," said Steve, so I wrote *P*, and behind me Carol said, "*Play* is *p, l, a, y,*" so I wrote that and finished the word myself.

"How about *is*?"

Lots of help with that one!

"Tell me what *sticky* starts with—two letters."

"*S, t,*" said Stephani. "Like me."

"Play Doh is sticky," I read the chart. "Read this with me." They did.

"Play Doh is sticky, says Kim," I said, adding "says Kim."

"You need quotation marks, now," Andrew informed me.

"Is Andrew right?" I asked the others. They agreed, so Andrew told me where to put those marks.

"Don't forget to say it's fun," Kim reminded us.

"Who can tell me how to write *but*?"

"*B, u, t,*" came several fast voices.

I wrote *its* and turned back to them with my eyebrows raised. "*Fun?*"

"*F, u, n!*" they chorused. "And a period!" called Ben.

So now it said: "Play Doh is sticky" says Kim but its fun.

"Are we all finished now?" I asked. Many hands shot up; we went on until it looked like this: "Play Doh is sticky," says Kim, "but its fun."

"Now is it all there?" I asked again.

Silence from some, yeses from some. Allison said, tentatively, "Is that *its* right?"

"Yes," Lori answered her positively. "I know about that. You don't need the apostrophe unless it tells about possession."

I kept still. Andrew raised his hand, also tentative. "I think it needs the apostrophe in this sentence," he said.

> **I was surprised that this problem had come up, but it had, so we would do more with it.**

A discussion went around about this for a minute or two, then they all looked at me. "Who is right?"

"I can tell you *what* is right," I offered, and I put the marker on the chart and put an apostrophe to make the word *it's*.

"Why?" challenged Lori.

"In this *it's*," I said to them all, "the apostrophe takes the place of the *i* in the word *is*. If Kim said her sentence v e r y s l o w l y we would hear 'it is fun.'"

They tried that out, saying it to themselves softly.

Then we read it all together and went on with the day. I made a mental note, and at recess a real note in my plans, that we needed to zero in on these *its*es as they appeared. I was surprised that this problem had come up, but it had, so we would do more with it.

My surprise—nearly incredulity—was because these were all young teachers-in-training. The *its*es of their childhoods, in their workbooks of isolated examples, had certainly not connected to them.

Language is an integral whole. You don't speak or write it in unrelated bits, you speak or write it whole. When children write in connected, continuous, personal wholes, they can also use their writing to dissect their language to find out how it goes together. If the dissected bits belong to them, they will care. With luck and good management, they will even be fascinated. They will even learn. Sometimes, I confess, I think it would be easier if I could just glue into everyone's brain the three kinds of *its* and be done with it. The trouble is, I'd have to glue in everything else, too, and there would never be any surprises, never any delights in the wacky way children learn. There would, indeed, be no wackiness anywhere, and perhaps no humanity.

Notes: Grammar as You Go

The children's own writing provides the class with the best examples for teaching the elements of standard English, such as grammar, spelling, usage, punctuation, phonics, noun-verb agreement, inflections, and all the other areas listed as "reading skills" and "writing skills" and even "thinking skills" in the basal readers. Keep a list of these elements that are required or necessary for the children you are teaching. When you need to teach a skill, look over the children's writings and find three illustrations of whatever it is. Having asked the writers first for permission:

- Write up the three samples on the board or overhead.
- Have the students read aloud ("Jamie, please read your sentence").
- Identify as a class the feature of the language that these quotations illustrate.
- Underline or highlight the feature in each sentence, or have three children do it if they can reach.
- Discuss how the feature works, generate the rule or a reasonable facsimile.
- Make the board (or chart or overhead) version correct
- Erase the correct part.
- Use the resulting fill-in-the-blank sentences for seatwork or homework.
- Keep a copy in the class file, which will become your class's English book.

For phonics review and teaching, write a class chart story every few days with an emphasis on the letter (most effective to begin with consonants) or blend. Then:

- Remind the class of what the phonics focus is for this chart.
- Ask for sentences to be dictated for you to write.

- Every couple of sentences have the story re-read ("Everyone whose socks are pink read the pink sentence").
- Read the whole thing chorally when it's finished.
- Choose a child to circle the element you're focusing on; that child will pass the marker to another child, and so on, until the chart has all its *k*s or *br*s or whatever circled.
- Count the elements on which you are focusing.
- Reduce this chart for the next day's seatwork or homework.
- Keep the reduced charts in the class English book.

12

The World Is Our Oyster

Math, Science, and the Rest of It

Talk, talk, talk, talk about it, talk it over, talk it through—this is what math is at the beginning. The first thing that has to happen at school is play. The Math Their Way people, as well as others who believe in and practice math-with-manipulatives, know this well and call it "exploration." When you aren't feeling and playing with something, you're talking about it, sharing discoveries out loud, child-to-child, child-to-grownup, or child-to-teacher. The first connection, to oral language, organically connects what the child is discovering through manipulation to her routine use of language.

> **Talk, talk, talk, talk about it, talk it over, talk it through—this is what math is at the beginning.**

Jessica, in first grade, was playing with some pattern blocks the other day and describing them out loud.

"These are the same," she said to me, holding up the blue diamond-shaped block and the orange square. "This is a square," she held up the blue one "because it has four sides." She counted the points, "1, 2, 3, 4. And this is a square, too," she said, counting the orange one's corners, "1, 2, 3, 4. They're the same, see?" she asked me. Then, assuming that I did, she explained further. "Except the blue one's lying down."

Jessica is in the process of learning to name and own the shapes and their words. First she is paying close attention to the blocks' shapes them-selves, and seeing their similarities and differences, talking about them in her own way, feeling them, connecting their difference particularly in language

> ## "Who can find things in this room that are square like the orange block?"

that makes a picture for her. After some time of this exploration, I can give Jessica the names—it would be best if she asked for them, but unless she needs them she probably won't ask. We can use these names, orally at first: "Who can find things in this room that are square like the orange block?" and then written: "Please help me describe the pattern Jessica and Ashley have made with the pattern blocks today. We'll make a chart about it." So we talk, and the chart ends up reading:

> Ashley and Jessica made a design with the pattern blocks. Cecily did a little but Ashley and Jessica did the most. There are fourteen yellow blocks in the center. They are hexagons. Hexagons have six sides. They put blue diamonds on all the edges of the hexagons that don't have another hexagon on them. The blue diamonds are called parallelograms. It looks like a sunflower with little blue leaves. The end.

This narrative is really using the written English language to connect in print the vocabulary of geometry to the children, as well as they are connected in speaking.

The same thing can be done with numbers and counting as with shapes. The class has been studying spiders, and went on a spider hunt walk the other day. When we came back, the students and I made a picture of what we had seen, and we each wrote a sentence about it (for example, "I saw a black spider. It has a web"). A few days later I asked them what we knew about the creatures and habitats we saw.

> ## "The spider has eight legs. The daddy-long-legs has six legs. Altogether it makes fourteen legs. 8 + 6 = 14."

"We saw," they dictated, "a black spider and a daddy-long-legs. It wasn't a black widow spider. The daddy-long-legs was brown. The spider has eight legs. The daddy-long-legs has six legs. Altogether it makes fourteen legs. $8 + 6 = 14$."

When we school people have thought of doing writing, or reading, in math, the first thing we have thought of is word problems. For a long time, that was the only thing we thought of. There are certainly many good things about word problems, in theory at any rate, such as that they teach "thinking skills" and blend the real world with the school-math world. But we've gone at them backward.

Actually, word problems come first, before the numerals are even thought of—in the real world, that is. That toddler gets to be four or five and is matching her dolls to her blankets or her dinosaur models to rocks, and there are four of one and six of another. She figures out that she needs two more to be even, and in figuring this out she has devised what is essentially a problem in subtraction, to find the difference. She puts this into her own, spoken language, not realizing that she is doing math. She is organically connected to the issue of the dolls and the blankets, so both her language and her number comparing are very meaningful to her. It has a context. Then Jessica, in school, learns to talk about the events and materials there that bring size and shape to the world, that invite understanding by comparison. She connects her oral language to these new uses, for herself. She owns this language and this connection.

Everything these two children do is a word problem.

There is a developmental sequence here. First the child is learning her language, learns to speak and reason and name. Simultaneously she is working with the elements of her world, playing with the blocks, constantly making and observing patterns, making comparisons about size, shape, and amount, and talking about them constantly. She puts her math experiences into language and doesn't differentiate between the language she uses to talk to her doll and the language she uses to talk about the number and shape of the leaves and blocks and dinosaurs she deals with every day.

Then reading and writing enter her life, in school usually, and she finds that the things that happen can be put into print on a chart. These charts can be about what cats do and "Our Trip to the Fire Station," and they can also be about designs with shapes and about spiders' legs. Then, only then, after the connection to English, does the language of math, the symbolic shorthand, come into her day. It can be an exciting new translation of things she has already learned how to talk about in words. Math is fascinating, and the fascination can shine through in either language.

It seems to me essential, then, to take the time to write down the discoveries and the questions the children invent for themselves to answer. This is simply more text, child-centered text, that the children can use to

> **Word problems come first, before the numerals are even thought of—in the real world, that is.**

record what they have mathematically thought. Students will also find useful and connecting either scribing their own thoughts or telling an adult what to scribe, either individually or in a group. Recording the ways in which mathematical hypotheses occur, are tested, and have solutions can begin with the youngest children, both in groups and personally. Later, a personal writing-to-learn journal in math will be a logical continuation of this work. Here again, just as in Gloria's class, the children who are not "good at math" will have a process in which they can be successful, and those who are not "good with language" will be able to show off their relative ease with math.

Numbers, numerals, and math operations aren't even part of the deal until a lot of exploration and play have happened in the early days of school. A lot of talk about numbers and operations, yes, but only as the environment or the moment requires. Rote counting and rhymes about numbers, and following the example of the Count, who counts nearly everything that goes down Sesame Street, are part of the fabric of the primary class. This work can be the stuff of writing and reading, as in the charts about designs and spider legs, so that rather than be afraid of or tensed for math, children—and teachers—can simply expect it and accept it without realizing that it's something separate and scary. (For such a long time math-in-school has been exclusively paper-and-pencil work and "do the odd-numbered problems on page 216 for homework," that teachers and children alike lost sight of the possibility that math was anything else. The school's sequence has been neatly in reverse: the numbers, the symbols, have been the focus first.)

> **Numbers merely act as the shorthand language for mathematical thoughts, just as words do for all our thoughts.**

Word problems have traditionally seemed to exist as another subject, separate from Math the Algorithmic Study. "If it doesn't have numbers it can't be math" is unfortunately what many children have been brought up to believe. They—both teachers and students—have been misled by our time-honored backward sequence into the belief that math *has* nothing but numbers. Most of us have completely lost sight of the reality, which is that numbers merely act as the shorthand language for mathematical thoughts, just as words do for all our thoughts.

What has so often happened in textbook-based math programs is just this backwards sequence. The math textbook, any elementary math textbook, asks children to do and make sense of word problems in the math book as a follow-up to several pages of algorithms, simply numbers. All those endless pluses and minuses, no matter if they are on a tear-out workbook page with bright cartoonlike pictures all around the edge or if they are stuck fast in a hardcover book with—maybe—one bit of colored illustration near the top or the bottom. These deadly pages are simply calculation practice. I have nothing against calculation practice, except that we've taught too many children—including me—that *that's* what math is.

And word problems have come, uselessly, after these pages and pages. Word problems have been used as illustrations of the algorithm, rather than the algorithm as notation for the problem first. There has been no organic connection, and, what's worse, there has been the implied message that these word problems should be more fun, should connect to the child.

The "If Johnny had three cookies in his lunch and gave one to Bill, how many would he have left?" problem comes in a section of the first-grade textbook on subtraction, after several pages of 3 - 1 = _____. Or, in many current texts, 3 - 1 = ☐ , with a box for the answer. (I don't know why a box. Probably it is a precursor to the horrible little ovals of the standardized tests.)

But problems to be solved mathematically surface in the life of the classroom community all the time. The jillions of lines we have to make are natural places to count and compare. "Who's got a red shirt? Red shirts line up first. How many red shirts are there?" Chorally count them, touching or pointing to each one. "Now who's wearing green? Greens line up, please. How many?" Count them. "What do we have more of today? How many more?" Or how many fewer? Begin to use the language that math problems have always been couched in, but do it often and orally for years before the same words are used in print. And long before the print is from an unrelated textbook, make your own. Write down on charts these same problems you and the class create, and read them (or "read" them), so that the idea belongs to the children. Math is as organically part of them as anything else their language describes for them.

> **"Who's got a red shirt? Red shirts line up first. How many red shirts are there?"**

The growing use of Math Their Way and similar hands-on programs has brought more and more conversation and logic and reasoning and words into the time for math, and in fact some elements of math appear all through the day. Since I have my eye out for integrating all the subject areas into a whole child I see them more often and capitalize on them as often as I can. I am continually finding myself doing comparisons, making graphs, and looking for patterns in places and moments I would formerly never have considered "math territory." Only after many days of work exploring and manipulating and talking and reading their own charted ideas and discoveries do the children begin to record for themselves. To transfer what their hands and eyes and voices know into a system of symbolic representation needs, as I have said, several steps; we have had them all out of order all these years.

At first this is a picture-symbol representation; if the child has been making patterns out of rocks or shells or cubes or whatever, she draws the pattern life-size on empty paper. The requirement for correctness here is the intrinsic one of whether the picture of the pattern and the pattern itself are the same: a pattern of blue block/red block/blue block/red block, for example, should look blue/red/blue/red on the paper. If the child has taken a small container of beans that are blue only on one side and tossed them onto a blank sheet of paper, she records the beans themselves by drawing three blue ones (those whose blue sides are up) and three white.

After we make a graph of fruits, for example, we can say things about it in either language. Suppose everyone has chosen to make a "real" graph, which means that there are real apples, grapes, bananas, oranges, and kiwis all lined up on a big paper on the floor ruled in a graph format. We can count how many of each kind we have, and write the numbers on the board if we want. We can look at the apples and the grapes and tell which is more and how we can find how much more. We can write this question and answer down as a problem: "How many more grapes are there than apples? There are seven apples and ten grapes. So there are three more grapes than apples. We counted from seven: eight, nine, ten, and there were three."

> **By this time nearly all the children have absorbed the most important concept of all: that math is fun, part of their lives, and they can do it.**

With any of these investigations, with unifix cubes, apples, or shirts, the final act can be a note, a sentence or two, a labeled illustration, in an investigations journal or a math log. In addition to making the connection between writing and math, between words and numbers, the math log sneakily gives children another place where they have to make numerals.

By this time nearly all the children have absorbed the most important concept of all: that math is fun, part of their lives, and they can do it. It is becoming more and more organically connected to them, in reading, talking, representational drawing, and finally in the symbolic numerals and operational signs. From this beginning it is only a matter of continuing in the same ways, continuing every year to connect the children to similar problems in their own lives so that they are connected to the strategy organically first. The same principle holds for science.

There were pumpkins everywhere, all with black-marker faces staring out in varying degrees of horrible. It was November 1, when pumpkins seem very dreary. All the witches and ballerinas and ghosts and Ninjas had gone to their yearly rest, but here were all these pumpkins still, all over the room. When the children came in that day, makeup scrubbed away, veins coursing with sugar, they were as put off as I was, so we had a discussion about what to do with them.

"Let them rot," said Robin, with a snarl through the word *rot*. Part of him was still Dracula from the night before.

"Yeah!" joined in Bobbie, eyes gleaming. "They'll be all gushy and gross."

Jane was squirming. "That would be disgusting," she said quietly. "Could we eat them instead?"

"Let's see now," I said, chalk in hand. "We could let them rot," I repeated as I wrote *rot* on the chalkboard, "or we could eat them," I said, writing *eat* under *rot*. "Any other choices?"

"We could just throw them away," said Harry.

"Yeah, that's what my mom does," said Michael.

"But that would be wasteful," said Jane precisely.

Throw away, I added to the list on the board. "Is it more wasteful to let them rot or to throw them away?" I asked.

Clamor of voices—"throw them!" "rot!" "rot!" "throw!"—until I put up my hand. "Now wait a minute," I said. "It's hard to think while you're shouting. Think, now, with your mouths closed. Which is more wasteful, to let them rot or to throw them away?"

Aaron's hand shot up, then Chris's, then, calmly, Jane's again.

"Aaron?"

"To throw them away," he said. "My mom always says to eat everything on my plate because to throw food away is wasteful."

Thank you, Aaron's mom, for that old-fashioned view! I thought.

"Yeah, but it's worse than that," Chris broke in, "to let them rot. They'll make germs and everything, Aaron, you know, all that moldy hairy stuff. My mom says that mold is bad for you. She cleans stuff out of the refrigerator all the time that's rotted, and she says that stuff would make me sick!"

"That would certainly be wasteful!" I teased him. "So when she cleans all that hairy stuff out of the refrigerator, Chris, where does she put it?"

Jane's hand was, uncharacteristically, waving madly in the air and her cheeks were puffed out with the self-imposed effort of not interrupting.

"In the garbage, of course," said Chris, smacking the palms of his hands down hard on his knees. "What else?"

"That's what I was going to say!" Jane burst out. "That's the same thing! If we let the pumpkins rot in here, it's just the same as if they rot on the dump! They're still wasted, either way, Chris's mom takes her garbage to the dump, too. I mean, either way, nobody can use them."

A silence fell, as everyone considered Jane's connection. I wrote *mold?* and *dump?* on the board during this silence.

"Well, but what are we going to do with ours?" This from Carla, the one who always wanted to know what was next on the agenda of the day.

> "Shall we read our three choices again?" I suggested, and, as I framed the words the group read out together "*rot, eat, throw away.*"

"Shall we read our three choices again?" I suggested, and, as I framed the words the group read out together "*rot, eat, throw away.*"

"Only it's really only two choices," Carla corrected us.

Michael got up, marched monster-stiff-legged over to the nearest pumpkin and picked it up. He looked at the group and then, with a lot of teeth showing, took a pretend bite out of the pumpkin.

"Eat them," he said simply, relaxing into his normal boy self.

"Shall we eat them?" I asked the class.

Various yesses and shrugs; then the important question emerged from several corners at once: How do you eat a pumpkin?

"We could make a pie," offered Cheryl.

I wrote *pie* on the board and waited.

"You can't eat pumpkins plain, like apples," said Robin, thinking aloud.

"I know, I know!" said Mary and Josh together, from opposite sides of the room. "*Seeds!*"

I turned to write *seeds* on the board, but it was clear the decision was being made without me.

"Toast them!"

"We'll need salt!"

"What do you like best, the inside or the shell?"

"If they get too brown they'll be yukky."

"I get to cut the top off mine!"

"We'll need lots of newspaper, you know." This, of course, from Jane.

I gave up on my list. It was definitely time for action. As we organized ourselves for this new task, it appeared that we had pleased both fastidious Jane and ghoulish Bobbie. Jane went to the closet for newspapers while Bobbie clasped her hands together and looked up at me soulfully.

"Oh, *Goody!*" she exclaimed. "We get to clean out the gushy stuff!"

Many teachers, perhaps most women elementary teachers, have a truly love-hate relationship with science. Any study of how science has been taught in elementary classrooms over the last forty years reveals paradoxes galore, and it seems that most of these paradoxes are rising up to our faces once again, much as rakes hidden in the summer grass rise up when we step on their tines. Bobbie doesn't have this problem. Follow Bobbie's lead.

Perhaps one of the most important things we do in school, then, is simply to rearrange what they have observed into some kind of shape, some paradigm or other.

When children come to school in the first place, at the earliest ages, they have already been observing their world for five or six years nonstop, every minute they are awake. There is such a tremendous amount to take in! Penni has spent countless days observing the biology of nature around her, deer tracks and chipmunks, tomato plants and dandelions. She has asked the names of all the animals and plants that have come into her field of vision, real and tele-. Jed has spent many hours in kitchens, his own and Grandma's, watching chemical reactions of various kinds. Some have been planned, as the thickening of the sauce for the spaghetti; some have not, as the discovery in the fridge of the spoiled meat that Mama was going to fix for supper. Sara and Sonny have watched their lobsterman father watch the sky and the wind and the water for nearly every day of their seven years. All these children, all children, absorb a lot of information, and also misinformation, about how their world, and all that sits in and on it, works.

The children have not been aware that they were doing science at these times, leave aside doing the various subgroups of science. Penni didn't know she was a biologist, Jed had no idea that chemistry abounded in his life, the twins never heard the word *meteorology*.

Perhaps one of the most important things we do in school, then, is simply to rearrange what they have observed into some kind of shape, some paradigm or other. Perhaps it is important for us to understand these differences, but not for the children. I don't know. I do know that they need to see the integration, and to experience the events, in order for them to continue in this world we have so busily fragmented. It's no help having experts on oak trees and elm trees and baobab trees if in the meantime no one cares about the forest. Children have to see that *we* care, that *we* are curious about our world.

Asking questions to extend our knowledge is usually the way we go with our curiosity; the younger we are the more we ask. This instinct is the driving force behind the relatively new idea of double-entry journals.

"First I tried to make the paper float," wrote Annie on the left side of her investigations notebook page, "and it did for a while but I thought it wood get soked and it did. The clay has to be rely thin and the edges curled up before it will float at all." And on the right side she wrote, "Tomorrow I'll try the foil and the waxed paper."

The experiments continued for a couple weeks with Annie's third-grade classroom. "I think my big foil boat will hold 10 pennys," Jameel wrote on the right side of his one day. On the left, reporting the day's work, he had noted that the little one held four, and that he had cut a piece of foil four by four inches instead of the "little" one's three by three.

These children are devising their own questions, creating the pace of their investigation, and following themselves, with writing, through their own experiments' devising and conducting. Their teacher knows that they will learn more by having to put their thoughts and conclusions and questions into words, and she will learn better what they have done, how connected they are to the principles of water buoyancy, and, incidentally, how their mastery of English phonics and sentence structure is coming along. They don't get answers from her, either, only questions and reality checks about what they have discovered themselves. She deals in *whys. Why?* makes connections, integrates information. I hope that the future holds many *whys* for and by children and their teachers.

One of the most secure ways to rivet and tie new information into ourselves is writing. Writing can be part of the initial stages of a class's contemplation of something, such as the pumpkin seed list. A web is another way to put down information, and can be a class activity, something small groups do, or something each child does alone.

On a different first-grade day, when the tarantula visited the classroom (in a tightly screened terrarium, I hasten to add), we made a big webbing of all the things we thought we knew about spiders.

Thick and fast the suggestions came, and I wrote them on a big piece of chart paper. First the names: brown recluse, black widow, tarantula, wolf spider. Then the odd facts, which I asked the offerer where to put: "Trapdoor spiders," said Matt, "have to keep their eggs covered when it rains." (That one was easy.) Baby spiders are born from eggs; they eat—all kinds of things, all of which went on the chart; wolf spiders bite, so do black widows, "So do brown recluses," said Ashley. "My aunt got bit by one."

"Shall we put Ashley's aunt on our web?" I asked. The consensus was no on that one. This paper, three feet square, was pretty well filled up in about ten minutes of intense conversation. Then we went over the parts and read them again, chorally, to be sure that we all remembered everything.

> **"Now, let's put some of this information into a piece of writing," I said. "Who has an idea for a good first sentence?"**

"Now, let's put some of this information into a piece of writing," I said. "Who has an idea for a good first sentence?" I was hanging another piece of paper, and when I turned around I nearly knocked Andrew over. He was standing right in front of me, holding out a blue marker.

"My sentence is first and it's terrific," he said. "'Black widow spiders and brown recluse spiders are deadly.'"

So I wrote that in blue, asking for a little help with spelling as always. The next sentence came from Kelly, and I wrote it in green; the next in brown, then a red, a purple, a black—a biiiig one—and finally orange. Each time I crossed out the relevant entry on the web, to show that we had used it already. The chart then looked like this:

> "Brown Recluse and Black Widow spiders are deadly. Some live underground and some live on the ground. Trap door spiders live in the sand and dirt. They have to keep their eggs covered in the rain. Babies come in an egg sac.
>
> "They eat all kinds of flies—butterflies, crane flies, wasps, hornets, bees, beetles, grasshoppers, small birds. Wolf spiders bite very hard."

As you see, we could have done this in any number of ways, and made a bigger deal about issues of paragraphing. In an older class I would have divided them into groups, assigned each group a spider, and asked them to write a web of their own spider first, then a set of questions they needed to get answers for. Then we would have made the text from the web, or not— probably they wouldn't have needed the model.

This group, Andrew, Matt, Ashley, Kelly, and their twenty-three class-mates, then worked in groups on a big piece of paper to illustrate one of these sentences and copy it onto the paper (that's why they were each in a different color). When we were all done there was quite an elegant class book about spiders that they could read at other times.

The ways writing can be connected to science are infinite if three questions are part of any inquiry:

1. What do we know? (make a web or a list)
2. What don't we know? (make a set of questions)
3. What can and will we work at finding out? (choose areas of study and write about them, for starters)

Take the information the children already have, in other words, give it room and validation, and go on from there, building and connecting the children and their information to their world, in their context.

> **Teaching, whether it is a synonym for education or not, is both art and science, and the ability to do it well requires immense confidence, intuition, knowledge, understanding, and curiosity.**

Popularly, it is believed that science somehow requires more brain than art or craft, that the mathematicians and physicists of the world have more usable intelligence than the writers and historians and linguists. Even I, who believe in my own brain, even I as I write this am in awe of mathematicians and physicists. It is in fact identical to my awe of car repairpeople and computer programmers. Perhaps awe is why educators and others call themselves "social scientists," so that they will fit into an erroneous and artificial classification. Teaching, whether it is a synonym for education or not, is both art and science, and the ability to do it well requires immense confidence, intuition, knowledge, understanding, and curiosity.

The very word *science*, though, comes from one of our many linguistic ancestors, Latin. In Latin it means, simply, "knowledge." Knowledge is the stuff of teaching and learning, in proportions and relationships personal to each human mind. We make it available in as many ways and as accurately as we can to the generations following us; what they do is theirs to do and we can only, finally, wish them well.

Bibliography

Ashton-Warner, Sylvia. 1963. *Teacher.* Simon and Shuster

Babbitt, Natalie. 1975. *Tuck Everlasting.* Farrar Straus Giroux.

Baker, Keith. 1990. *Who Is the Beast?* Harcourt Brace Jovanovich.

Baylor, Byrd. 1974. *Everybody Needs a Rock.* Aladdin Books.

Biklen, Douglas, and Michele Sokoloff, eds. 1978. *What Do You Do When Your Wheelchair Gets a Flat Tire?* Scholastic.

Bourgeois, Paulette. 1986. *Franklin in the Dark.* Scholastic.

Brown, Margaret Wise. 1942. *The Runaway Bunny.* Harper Trophy.

Buckley, Richard. 1985. *The Greedy Python.* Picture Book Studio.

Burke-Weiner, Kimberly. 1992. *The Maybe Garden.* Beyond Words.

Byars, Betsy. 1970. *The Summer of the Swans.* Viking.

Calkins, Lucy. 1983. *Lessons from a Child.* Heinemann Educational Books.

———. 1986. *The Art of Teaching Writing.* Heinemann Educational Books.

———. 1992. *Living between the Lines.* Heinemann.

Carle, Eric. 1977. *The Grouchy Ladybug.* Crowell.

———. 1989a. *Animals, Animals.* Scholastic.

———. 1989b. *The Very Hungry Caterpillar.* Putnam.

"A Conversation with Lisa Delpit." *Language Arts* vol. 68 (Nov. 1991).

Cowley, Joy. 1980. *Mrs. Wishy-Washy.* Shortland.

———. 1983a. *Dan the Flying Man.* Shortland.

———. 1983b. *In a Dark Dark Wood.* Shortland.

Cronn, Lynessa. Personal conversation, 12 August 1991.

DeClements, Barthe. 1985. *Sixth Grade Can Really Kill You.* Scholastic.

Delpit, Lisa. 1991. "Skills and Other Dilemmas of a Progressive Black Educator." *Harvard Educational Review* vol. 56, no. 4.

Dorris, Ellen. 1991. *Doing What Scientists Do.* Heinemann.

Eastman, P. D. 1960. *Are You My Mother?* Random House, Beginner Books.

Gackenbach, Dick. 1977. *Harry and the Terrible Whatzit.* Houghton Mifflin.

Gilbert, Anne Green. 1977. *Teaching the Three Rs through Movement Experiences.* Macmillan.

———. 1992. *Creative Dance for All Ages.* American Alliance for Health, Physical Education, Recreation, and Dance.

Gould, Stephen Jay. 1981. *The Mismeasure of Man.* W. W. Norton.

Graves, Donald. 1983. *Writing: Teachers and Children at Work.* Heinemann.

Heath, Shirley Brice. 1983. *Ways with Words.* Cambridge University Press.

Johnson, Katie. 1987. *Doing Words.* Houghton Mifflin.

Johnson, Terry, and Daphne Louis. 1987. *Literacy through Literature.* Heinemann.

Koch, Kenneth. 1970. *Rose, Where Did You Get That Red?* Harper and Row.

Lasker, Joe. 1980. *Nick Joins In*. Albert Whitman.

L'Engle, Madeline. 1971. *A Wrinkle in Time*. Dell Yearling.

LeSeig, Theo. 1961. *Ten Apples up on Top*. Random House.

MacLachlan, Patricia. 1980. *Through Grandpa's Eyes*. Harper Trophy.

———. 1985. *Sarah, Plain and Tall*. Harper and Row.

Mayer, Mercer. 1985. *There's a Nightmare in my Closet*. Dial.

Milne, A. A. 1961. *When We Were Very Young*. Dutton.

Minarik, Elsie. 1964. *Little Bear's Visit*. Harper Trophy.

Munsch, Robert. 1980. *The Paper Bag Princess*. Annick.

Munsch, Robert, and Michael Kusugak. 1988. *A Promise Is a Promise*. Annick.

Murray, Donald. 1968. *A Writer Teaches Writing*. Houghton Mifflin.

O'Neill, Mary. 1961. *Hailstones and Halibut Bones*. Doubleday.

Paulsen, Gary. 1987. *Hatchet*. Puffin Books.

———. 1990. *Canyons*. Puffin Books.

Peterson, Jeanne W. 1977. *I Have a Sister, My Sister Is Deaf*. Harper Trophy.

Rief, Linda. 1991. *Seeking Diversity*. Heinemann.

Riekenhof, Lottie L. 1978. *The Joy of Signing*. Gospel.

Roberts, Willo Davis. 1980. *The Girl with the Silver Eyes*. Scholastic.

———. 1988. *Megan's Island*. Aladdin Books.

Ruef, Kerry. 1992. *The Private Eye*. The Private Eye.

Seuss. 1968. *The Foot Book*. Random House, Bright and Early Books.

Shaw, Charles. 1947. *It Looked Like Spilt Milk*. Harper.

Silverstein, Shel. 1964. *The Giving Tree*. Harper and Row.

———. 1976. *A Light in the Attic*. Harper and Row.

Smith, Frank. 1985. *Reading without Nonsense*. 2nd ed. Teachers College Press.

Sonneborn, Ruth. 1987. *Friday Night Is Papa Night*. Viking Penguin, Picture Puffins.

Steinbergh, Judith. 1983. *Beyond Words: Writing Poetry with Children*. Wampeter.

Stevenson, James. 1984. *Worse than Willy*. Greenwillow.

Stinson, Kathy. 1982. *Red Is Best*. Annick Press.

Strongin, Herb. 1976. *Science on a Shoestring*. Addison Wesley.

Viorst, Judith. 1972. *Alexander and the Terrible, Horrible, No-Good, Very Bad Day*. Macmillan, Aladdin Books.

Voigt, Cynthia. 1981. *Homecoming*. Fawcett Juniper.

———. *Dicey's Song*. Fawcett Juniper.

Ward, Cindy. 1988. *Cookie's Week*. Scholastic.

Wassermann, Selma, and George Ivany. 1988. *Who's Afraid of Spiders? Teaching Elementary Science*. Harper and Row.

———. 1990. *Serious Players in the Primary Classroom*. Teachers' College Press.

White, E. B. 1952. *Charlotte's Web*. Harper and Row.

Wilder, Laura Ingalls. 1971. *Little House in the Big Woods*. Harper and Row, Harper Trophy.

Wildsmith, Brian. 1982. *The Cat on the Mat*. Oxford University Press.

Williams, Vera B. 1982. *A Chair for My Mother*. Mulberry Books.

Add these resources to your program today!

Here's a whole year's worth of literature-based units!

Month by Month with Children's Literature
Your K–3 Curriculum for Math, Science, Social Studies, and More
by Margaret Bryant, Marjorie Keiper, and Anne Petit
Inspire your students to learn through literature.

Reach all students with lessons that teach basic skills within 10 literature-based units. This comprehensive curriculum takes you through the entire school year with strategies for developing and implementing mandated curriculum. You'll have complete lessons to effectively integrate all content areas.

ZB57-W . . . $59

Multicultural stories from around the globe promote reading, drawing, and imagining
Folktales
Teaching Reading through Visualization and Drawing
by Laura Rose
Grades K–5

Invite your students into reading and imagining with folktales from various cultures.

Folktales presents 10 traditional multicultural stories. Each story offers a drawing page with each page of text. Children visualize and draw the events of each story as you read it aloud or play the tapes.

123 pages, 8 1/2" x 11", softbound.
ZB29-W . . . $15.95

Folktales Audiotapes
Let author Laura Rose read for you! The taped stories add songs and musical instruments from the country of origin of each tale. Five audiotapes, with one complete story on each side; durable vinyl storage case.

ZA03-W . . . $32.95

Order both the Folktales book and 5 audiotapes and save $5.00.

Z010-W . . . $43.90

CALL, WRITE, OR FAX FOR YOUR FREE CATALOG!

- -

ORDER FORM ☎ Please include your phone number in case we have questions about your order.

Qty.	Item #	Title	Unit Price	Total
	ZB57-W	Month by Month	$59	
	ZB29-W	Folktales	$15.95	

Name _____

Address _____

City _____

State _____ Zip _____

Phone (_____) _____

Method of payment (check one):

❏ Check or Money Order ❏ Visa

❏ MasterCard ❏ Purchase Order attached

Credit Card No. _____

Expires _____

Signature _____

Subtotal	
Sales Tax (AZ residents, 5%)	
S & H (10% of Subtotal)	
Total (U.S. Funds only)	

CANADA: add 22% for S& H and G.S.T.

100% SATISFACTION GUARANTEE

Upon receiving your order you'll have 90 days of risk-free evaluation. If you are not 100% satisfied, return your order within 90 days for a 100% refund of the purchase price. No questions asked!

To order, write or call:

Zephyr Press

REACHING THEIR HIGHEST POTENTIAL

P.O. Box 66006-W
Tucson, AZ 85728-6006
(520) 322-5090
FAX (520) 323-9402